# Tom Hutchinson

*elementary*

## new HOTLINE

*student's book*

### Key to symbols

▶1.2  Look at this part of the Grammar reference section, on pages 101 -107.

Ω  This is a learning to learn activity.

## Oxford University Press

# Contents

**1** Explore *New Hotline*. **Look through the book. Where do you find these things?**

the Contents page
Pronunciation practice
the Grammar reference
the Wordlist

**2** **a** Look at these people. Do you know them? Look quickly through the story on page 4 and find their names.

**b** You won't find one of the girls' names in this unit. Look through the book. Can you find her name?

THE ORIGINAL
SIGHTSEEING TOUR

**VICTORIA ROAD**

THE ORIGINAL
SIGHTSEEING TOUR

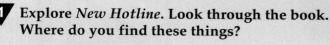

---

### Learning objectives

**Victoria Road:** Revision
Introducing the characters

**Language work:** Revising tenses ▶I.1–2, I.4–5
Giving personal information ▶I.3

# Sue's penfriend

## 1 Look at the story.

a Where are the people?

b Who is the girl in the photograph?

c What is Sue doing?

d Why is Sue angry at the end?

Speech bubbles in photo 1:
Hello, Mrs Scott. Is Vince in?
Hello, Terry. Hello, Casey. Come in.

Speech bubbles in photo 2:
What are you doing?
I'm writing a letter to my new penfriend.

## 2 🔊 Now listen and follow in your book.

**Terry** Hello, Mr Scott. Hello, Mrs Scott. Is Vince in?

**Mrs Scott** Hello, Terry. Hello, Casey. Come in. Vince was upstairs just now. Vince!

**Vince** Hi, Tel. Is Casey with you?

**Terry** He's outside. Have you got your money?

**Vince** Oh no, I haven't. Hang on a minute.

**Sue** How do you spell your surname, Terry? Has it got an 'e' at the end?

**Terry** It's M – double O–R–E. Why? What are you doing?

**Sue** I'm writing a letter to my new penfriend.

**Terry** When did you get your computer?

**Sue** My grandma and grandpa bought it for my birthday last week. Now ssh! I'm trying to concentrate.

**Terry** What's the penfriend's name, Kamala?

**Kamala** Carmen. She's from Spain. I've got a photo here. Look. That's Carmen with her mum and dad and her brother. They're outside their flat.

**Terry** Mmm. She's very pretty. I like long hair.

**Sue** She hasn't got long hair now. It's short like mine.

**Terry** Oh, that's a pity. I don't like girls with short hair.

**Sue** Thank you very much, Terry Moore. Well, I don't like boys with small brains and big mouths. So don't be rude.

**Terry** What? Oh, er I'm sorry, Sue. I didn't mean…

**Casey** Come on, Terry, Vince. The bus is coming. Hurry up.

**Vince** Bye.

**Terry** Bye.

**Kamala** See you.

**Sue** 'I don't like girls with short hair.' He's such a fool, that Terry Moore, and so rude.

**Kamala** Oh, he's all right, Sue. Don't worry about it.

## Useful expressions

**5** How do you say these expressions in your language?

**Come in.**

**just now**

**Come on.**

**Hang on a minute.**

**Don't be rude.**

**Hurry up.**

**See you.**

**6** a Work in groups of three. One person is Terry, one is Sue, and one is all the others.

b Read the dialogue.

**3** Answer these questions.

a Where is Vince when Terry arrives?

b What are Sue and Kamala doing?

c Who is Carmen?

d Who is in the photograph?

e What does Terry like about Carmen?

f Why is Sue annoyed?

— optional activity —

**4** Close your book. Listen again.

— optional activity —

**FOLLOW UP**

**7** Put this conversation in the correct order.

A She's my penfriend.
B Who are the other people in the photograph?
C I'm writing a letter to Carmen.
D She's from Spain.
E What are you doing, Sue?
F Oh. Where's she from?
G They're Carmen's mum and dad. The boy is her brother.
H Yes, here you are.
I Who's Carmen?
J Have you got a photograph of her?

# LANGUAGE WORK

## Revising tenses ►I.1–2, I.4–5

 **1 Look at the Victoria Road story again.**

**a** Find more examples of these tenses. Make a list for each one.

| present simple | present continuous | past simple |
|---|---|---|
| do you? | I'm writing | bought |

**b** Look at your list and find two questions, two negative verbs, and three short forms.

Examples
- question — *Is Vince in?*
- negative verb — *I don't like*
- short form — *haven't*

 **2 a Complete the sentences with these words. Some of them are used more than once.**

| are | he | my | her | is | am | his |
|---|---|---|---|---|---|---|
| have got | | from | our | | has got | don't |
| has | a | | him | | their | |

1 .......... you Spanish? No, I .......... from Argentina.

2 She .......... tall and she .......... short hair.

3 Casey and Vince .......... sixteen years old.

4 I .......... like Terry. .......... is such a fool.

5 Vince .......... a sister. .......... name .......... Susan. Terry .......... not got any brothers or sisters.

6 Carmen .......... writing a letter to .......... penfriend in England.

7 I .......... a penfriend. He is .......... Brazil. This is a photograph of .......... with .......... brother. They are in .......... kitchen.

8 Here is .......... photograph of .......... family. We .......... in .......... garden.

**b Change the verbs to short forms where possible.**

# Giving personal information
►I.3

 **3**  **Sue is on the telephone. She is talking to someone at the penfriend agency. Listen to their conversation.**

**a** Here are Sue's answers write the questions.

- Susan Scott.
- S–C–O– double T.
- In Hartfield.
- 18 Victoria Road.
- HA6 4BJ
- (01386) 754921
- Sixteen.
- 12th September.

**b** Listen again and check your answers.

**c** Work in pairs. Use the questions from Sue's interview. Interview your partner.

**d** Introduce your partner to the class.
*This is . . .*
*His/Her name is . . .*

──── optional activity ────

**FOLLOW UP**

**4 Write your own conversation with the penfriend agency.**

──────────

# Main grammar point:
## The present simple tense

*I don't get up early on Saturdays. I stay in bed. What do you do?*

*Casey doesn't stay in bed.*

*What does he do?*

*He plays football.*

*daily life*

**1**

## Learning objectives

| | |
|---|---|
| **Learning to learn:** | Learning grammar |
| **Victoria Road:** | Describing daily life ▶ 1.2<br>Giving commands and suggestions |
| **Language work:** | Telling the time ▶ 1.1<br>The present simple tense:<br>positive and negative statements ▶ 1.2–3 |
| **Reading:** | Finding information |
| **Listening:** | Listening for personal details<br>Understanding and expressing likes and dislikes |
| **Interaction:** | The present simple tense: questions |
| **Guided writing:** | What can you write about? |

 **Learning to learn: *Learning grammar***

Look through the unit. Find the Learning to learn activities. Which of these things does each activity have?

- a rule of use
- opportunities to use the tense
- simple examples of the tense
- tables to show how we form the tense
- practice activities

What other things can help you to learn grammar? Discuss your ideas.

# Terry's problem

**1** Look at the picture story. Complete these sentences with the correct subjects.

a ............. is bored.
b ............. tells Terry to get up.
c ............. has got nothing to do.
d ............. plays the guitar.
e ............. doesn't stay in bed late.
f ............. helps in her parents' shop.
g ............. phoned Terry.

> I'm bored. Every day's the same. I feel like a robot.

**2** 📼 Listen and follow in your book.

**Terry** I'm bored. Every day's the same. I feel like a robot. I get up at ten to eight, I get dressed, I have my breakfast, I go to school at twenty to nine, I come home at half past three, I do my homework, I watch TV, I get undressed and I go to bed at quarter past ten. And then the next day, I get up again at ten to eight, I get dressed, I…

**Mrs Moore** Come on, Terry. It's time you were up.

**Terry** What's the time?

**Mrs Moore** It's twenty-five past eleven. You can't stay in bed all day. Now get up. And make your bed, too.

**Later**

**Terry** What time is dinner, Mum?

**Mrs Moore** Dinner is at six o'clock. It's only five to two. What's the matter with you today?

**Terry** I've got nothing to do.

**Mrs Moore** Why don't you help me? You can tidy your room, or wash up, or iron some clothes, or go to the shops for me.

**Terry** Oh, Mum. I don't want to do housework.

**Mrs Moore** Go out, then.

**Terry** There's nothing to do around here.

**Mrs Moore** Other people do things. Look at Casey. He doesn't stay in bed till half past eleven at the weekend. He gets up early and plays football on Saturday mornings. And in the afternoon he washes the car or goes swimming.

**There's nothing to do around here.**

**Other people do things. Look at Casey. He doesn't stay in bed till half past eleven at the weekend.**

④

**What about Sue?**

**Er, no. Er… she does her community work at the hospital on Saturdays.**

⑤

**Well that's funny because she phoned you this morning.**

⑥

**Terry**  Yes, well, I don't like sport – except on TV.

**Mrs Moore**  You're lazy. That's your problem, Terry. Now I don't want you in my way. Go and see one of your friends.

**Terry**  I can't. They all do things on Saturdays. Casey plays football, Vince has guitar lessons, Kamala helps in her parents' shop.

**Mrs Moore**  What about Sue?

**Terry**  (blushing) Er, no. Er…she does her community work at the hospital on Saturdays.

**Mrs Moore**  Well, that's funny because she phoned you this morning.

### What do you think?

a  What is Terry's problem?

b  What can he do?

▼ **3** Answer these questions.

  a  What's the time when the story starts?

  b  Why isn't Terry at school?

  c  What does Mrs Moore suggest?

  d  What does Casey do on Saturdays?

  e  Why doesn't Terry play football?

  f  What does Sue do on Saturdays?

  g  What does Terry draw in his book?

— optional activity —

 **4**  **Close your book. Listen again.**

## Useful expressions

▼ **5** How do you say these expressions in your language?

**in my way**

  **Why don't you…**

    **It's time you were up.**

      **I've got nothing to do.**

  **What's the matter with you?**

**There's nothing to do around here.**

▼ **6**  a  Work in pairs. One person is Terry and the other is Mrs Moore.

  b  Read the dialogue.

— optional activity —

**FOLLOW UP**

▽ **7**  **Describe Terry's day.**

    Example
    *Terry gets up at ten to eight. He…*

# LANGUAGE WORK

## Telling the time ▶1.1

 **1** Look at these clocks and watches. What's the time?

 **2** Work in pairs.

**A** Ask 'What's the time?'
**B** Choose one of the times above and say it.

Example
**A** *What's the time?*
**B** *It's five past eight.*
**A** Point to the correct clock or watch.

**3** Look at these times.

| | | | |
|---|---|---|---|
| 18:15 | 3:45 | 7:30 | 6:55 |
| 7:40 | 18:50 | 6:20 | 8:20 |
| 2:45 | 8:50 | 16:20 | 7:55 |

**a** Say the times in digital form and in analogue form.

Example
18:15
*eighteen fifteen*
*quarter past six*

**b** 📼 Listen. Which of the times do you hear? What happens at each time?

##  The present simple tense ▶1.2–3

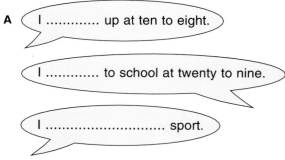 **4 a** Complete these sentences. Use the Victoria Road story on page 8 to help you.

**A** I ............. up at ten to eight.

I ............. to school at twenty to nine.

I ........................... sport.

**B** Casey ........... up early on Saturday mornings.

Casey ........... swimming.

Casey ...................... in bed till half past eleven.

**b** Look at the sentences in 4a. Can you see the differences between the sentences in A and B?

**c** Use these words to complete the tables.

plays   like   likes   play

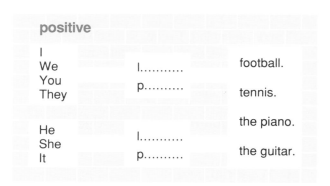

**positive**

| I We You They | l........... p.......... | football. tennis. |
|---|---|---|
| He She It | l........... p.......... | the piano. the guitar. |

**negative**

| I We You They | don't | l........ | football. tennis. |
|---|---|---|---|
| He She It | doesn't | p........ | the piano. the guitar. |

> This is the 'present simple' tense. We use it to talk about regular activities.

## 5

a **Think about your family. Write down three things which:**

- all the people in the family do.
- only you do.
- only your mother does.
- only your father does.

b **Compare your list with your partner's.**

**FOLLOW UP**

## 6

**Look at these opening times. Read the clues below. Match the opening times to the buildings.**

**A**

**Opening Times**
**Tuesday–Sunday**
**from 10.00–6.00**
*closed every Monday*

**B**

*Opening Hours*
**Monday–Friday**
**9.00–12.30 and 2.00–5.30**
**Saturday**
**9.00–12.30**
**Sunday Closed**

**C**

Opening hours
Monday–Saturday
8.00–8.00
Sunday
9.00–6.00

*Hours of Business*
*Monday–Friday*
*9.30–4.30*

**D**

The bank doesn't open every day.
The shop opens before the museum.
The post office doesn't open on Sundays.
The museum and the bank don't close at lunchtime.
The bank opens for five days a week.

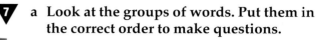

# The present simple tense: questions ▶1.4

## 7

a **Look at the groups of words. Put them in the correct order to make questions.**

tennis   you   play   do   ?

Sue   does   where   live   ?

b **Complete this chart. Use four of these words.**

do   likes   play   does   plays   like

| | | |
|---|---|---|
| ......... | I we you they | ......... |

football?
tennis?
the piano?
the guitar?

| | | |
|---|---|---|
| ......... | he she | ......... |

c **How do we make questions in the present simple tense?**

## 8

**Work in pairs. Use the cues. Ask about Casey. Then ask your partner about him/herself.**

Examples
*Does Casey like sport?*
*Yes, he does.*
*Do you like sport?*
*Yes, I do./No, I don't.*

like sport
stay in bed late on Saturdays
wash the car
play football
watch TV on Saturday afternoons
work in a shop
go swimming

**FOLLOW UP**

## 9

**Use the cues in Exercise 8. Write three sentences for each: one about Terry, one about Casey and one about yourself.**

Example
*Terry doesn't like sport.*
*Casey likes sport.*
*I like/don't like sport.*

# READING

 **a Read these questions.**

1 Can sleepwalkers see?

2 What did the girl from Wales do?

3 How much sleep do teenagers need?

4 What kinds of things do sleepwalkers do?

**b Look at the text. In which paragraph will you find the answer to each question?**

## Sleep Sleep Sleep

In a normal life a person sleeps for about twenty-five years. But why do we sleep? The simple answer is: we don't know. We need more sleep when we are young. A baby sleeps for about ten hours. A teenager sleeps for eight and a half hours and an adult for seven or eight hours. Old people need only five or six hours.

Do you ever talk or walk in your sleep? Sleepwalkers do amazing things. They open doors and windows, they ride bicycles and drive cars. They cook, they take a bath or a shower (often in their pyjamas), they shave, they clean their teeth, they get dressed, they dig the garden, and they get into bed with other people.

A man in Scotland woke up in his car two miles from his house. He had no clothes on. A girl from Wales woke up at five o'clock in the morning in a launderette. She had a shopping bag and the family's dog with her.

Sleepwalkers are asleep, but they have their eyes open and they can see. They can't wake up easily. If they do, they can't remember anything. Do you ever sleepwalk? Are you sure? Perhaps you do, but nobody sees you.

 **Right, Wrong or Don't know?**

|  | ✓ | ✗ | ? |
|---|---|---|---|
| a Everyone sleeps for eight hours a night. | ❑ | ❑ | ❑ |
| b Teenagers need less sleep than adults. | ❑ | ❑ | ❑ |
| c Some people sleep for only one or two hours. | ❑ | ❑ | ❑ |
| d The man from Scotland woke up at five o'clock in the morning. | ❑ | ❑ | ❑ |
| e The girl from Wales was in her pyjamas. | ❑ | ❑ | ❑ |
| f Sleepwalkers can't see. | ❑ | ❑ | ❑ |
| g Sleepwalkers remember everything they do | ❑ | ❑ | ❑ |

 **Which of these is not in the text?**

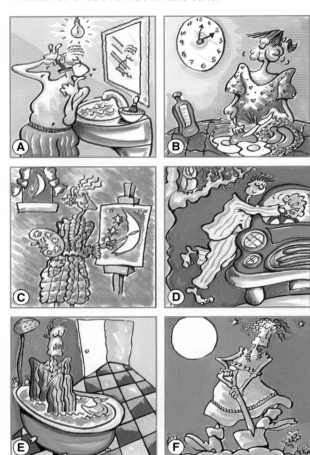

| **W O R D** | **W O R K** |

 **Find the verbs to complete these expressions.**

a ....... a shower      f ........ the door

b ....... a bicycle      g ....... up

c ....... your teeth     h ....... into bed

d ....... the garden     i ........ dressed

e ....... a car          j ........ the window

— optional activity —

**FOLLOW UP**

 **Answer these questions in full sentences.**

a How long do you sleep every day?

b Can you remember your dreams?

c What do you dream about?

d Do you snore?

e Do you talk in your sleep?

f Do you sleepwalk? If yes, what do you do?

# LISTENING

## Views of Britain

 **1** **Discuss these questions.**

   **a** What do you know about Britain?

   **b** Look at the pictures. What do they show?

 **2** 📼 **You will hear someone talking about Britain. First listen and find this information about the speaker.**

   **a** What is her name?

   **b** Where is she from?

   **c** Why is she in England?

 **3** **Work in pairs.**

   **a** Make a chart like this.

| likes | dislikes |
|-------|----------|
|       |          |
|       |          |

   **b** Listen again and fill in your chart.

   **c** Say what Paola likes and doesn't like.

— optional activity —

 **4** **What do you think people like or don't like about your country? Write down some ideas.**

— optional activity —

## FOLLOW UP

**5** **Complete this interview.**

**Interviewer** What do you like ......... England?

**Paola** I like the ............ . They are very friendly.

**Interviewer** ............... don't you like?

**Paola** I ............... like the weather. It's too ............... for me. And your times are all ............... .

**Interviewer** What ............... you mean?

**Paola** Well, you ............ at the wrong times. At my ...............school we have ............... at half ............... twelve. But I'm not ............... then. In my country I eat ............... three o'clock and then I ............... a rest. Here ............... England I have lessons in the afternoon, but ............... tired and I want ............... sleep. And then everything ............... very early. All the ............... close at half past five and ............... the restaurants and pubs ............... at eleven ............... or half past ten ............... night. But I love your ............... , and English breakfasts ............... great.

## INTERACTION

# Do you know your friends?

 **1** **Look at the rules for present simple questions in the Grammar reference (1.4).**

**a** Which of these verbs do not follow the rule?

to be   to go   to have got   can   to want

**b** How do we make questions with the verbs that do not follow the present simple rule?

 **2** **What do you know about your classmate?**

**a** Look at the questionnaire below.

| | |
|---|---|
| **1** | Has he/she got any brothers or sisters? |
| **2** | When does he/she get up? |
| **3** | What does he/she eat for breakfast? |
| **4** | What sports does he/she play? |
| **5** | Can he/she play a musical instrument? |
| **6** | What do his/her parents do? |
| **7** | What is his/her favourite subject? |
| **8** | Has he/she got a pet? |
| **9** | What job does he/she want to do? |
| **10** | What time does he/she go to bed? |
| **11** | When is his/her birthday? |

**b** Make a chart like this.

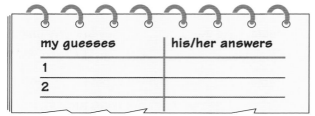

| my guesses | his/her answers |
|---|---|
| 1 | |
| 2 | |

**c** Find a partner. Try to answer the questions about him/her. Write your guesses in column 1 of your chart, 'my guesses'. Don't show it to your partner!

**d** Now ask your partner the questions and write his/her answers in column 2.

**e** Compare your guesses and the answers.

--- optional activity ---

**FOLLOW UP**

 **3** **Write the answers to the questionnaire for yourself and your friend.**

> Example
> *I have got two brothers and one sister. My friend has got two sisters.*

► Pronunciation: page 96

## GUIDED WRITING

# What can you write about?

 **1** **Before you write anything you should decide what you will write about.**

**a** Look at the pattern for a letter below. What can you put in each part?

**b** Note down some information and questions.

 ## *My life*

**2** **Write a letter to a new penfriend. Tell him/ her about your life and ask questions about his/her life. Follow this pattern.**

| |
|---|
| (your address)<br>(the date)<br><br>*Dear* (name)<br><br>*Hi. I'm your new penfriend. My full name is ...*<br>(Give some information about you and your family. Ask some questions.)<br><br>(Describe your daily life. Ask some questions.)<br><br>(Tell him/her about your likes/dislikes, your favourite things etc. Ask some questions.)<br><br>*I hope to hear from you soon.*<br>*Bye for now,*<br>(Your name) |

# Learning *diary* 1

**What have you learnt in this unit?**

**A** Do the self-check in the Workbook. Check any grammar problems in the reference section on pages 101–107, or ask your teacher.

**B** Look back at the unit. What activities did you do to revise the present simple tense? What can you do now to make sure that you remember the tense?

**Complete your learning diary.**

# Main grammar point:
## The past simple tense

*Where were you last night?*

*I was at a pop concert.*

*Did you go on your own?*

*No, I went with a friend.*

*Was the concert good?*

*No, I didn't like it. The singer wasn't very good.*

## Learning objectives

| | |
|---|---|
| **Learning to learn:** | Using reference sections |
| **Victoria Road:** | Talking about past events |
| **Language work:** | The past simple tense: 'to be' – statements and questions ▶ 2.1–2 |
| | The past simple tense: regular and irregular verbs ▶ 2.3–4 |
| | The past simple tense: negative ▶ 2.5 |
| **Reading:** | Reading and writing about a person's life-story |
| | The past simple tense: irregular verbs ▶ 2.4 |
| **Listening:** | Listening and taking notes |
| **Interaction:** | The past simple tense: questions ▶ 2.5 |
| **Guided writing:** | Paragraphs |

## Q Learning to learn: *Using reference sections*

a   Find these things. What pages are they on?

  ● the Grammar reference      ● the Wordlist
  ● the Contents pages         ● Useful sets

b   Turn to the grammar reference. Find these things.

  ● the grammar for this unit   ● comparatives and superlatives

c   Find the past simple tense again. What is each section about?

# Sue teases Terry

**1** **Look at the picture story.**

**a** Answer the questions.

   1 Who are the people?

   2 Where are they?

   3 What day is it?

**b** Are these sentences Right or Wrong?

   1 Casey had a good weekend.

   2 Sue and Kamala painted Sue's bedroom.

   3 Terry helped Sue.

   4 Terry was ill at the weekend.

   5 Terry likes the leisure centre.

   6 Sue doesn't like Terry.

**2** **Listen and follow in your book.**

**Kamala** Hi. Did you have a good weekend?

**Casey** Yes, it was great.

**Kamala** What did you do?

**Casey** I played football at the leisure centre on Saturday morning. In the afternoon I washed my dad's car and then I went swimming. What about you?

**Sue** We had a good time, too, didn't we, Kamala? We painted my bedroom. We had a good laugh.

**Terry** I thought you worked in your parents' shop on Saturdays, Kam.

**Kamala** Sue helped me in the shop in the morning, but we weren't very busy in the afternoon. So I helped her with her bedroom.

**Casey** Did you help, Tel?

**Sue** Oh no. Terry was ill, weren't you, Terry?

**Terry** No, I wasn't.

**Sue** That's strange. I phoned you at eleven o'clock and your mum said you were in bed. So I thought that you were ill.

**Kamala** Don't tease him, Sue.

**Terry** Oh, very funny. I didn't get up, because I didn't want to. I wanted to stay in bed. Anyway, I watched a film on television and listened to my records. All right?

**Casey** What was wrong, Tel?

**Kamala** It's all right, Casey. Terry wasn't ill. Sue's only kidding.

Casey  Why didn't you come to the leisure centre?

Terry  I'm fed up with that stupid leisure centre. It's for kids.

Casey  What's the matter with him?

Kamala  I think he fancies Sue, but she teases him all the time. It's funny, because she likes him really.

**What do you think?**

a  Does Terry like Sue?

b  Does Sue like Terry?

c  How can Casey and Kamala help?

 a  **What did Casey, Kamala, Sue and Terry do at these times:**

on Saturday morning?
on Saturday afternoon?

b  **What does Terry think about:**

the leisure centre?
Sue?

──────── optional activity ────────

 **Close your book. Listen again.**

17

## Useful expressions

**5** How do you say these expressions in your language?

**Oh, very funny.**

**I didn't want to.**

**She's only kidding.**

**We had a good laugh.**

**I'm fed up with . . .**

**He fancies Sue.**

**It's for kids.**

**6** a Work in groups of four. Each person takes one of the parts.

b Read the dialogue.

─── optional activity ───

**FOLLOW UP**

**7** Complete Kamala's diary.

**Saturday**

I _____ in the shop in _____ morning. Sue helped me. We _____ very busy _____ the afternoon, so Sue and I _____ her bedroom. We _____ a good laugh.

**Sunday**

I got _____ late and did _____ homework. After lunch Sue _____ . We went to the _____ centre and we _____ badminton.

**Monday**

I went to _____ with Sue. We met _____ and Casey at the _____ stop. Casey played football _____ the leisure centre at the _____ . Terry _____ do anything. He _____ in bed all morning and _____ television in the afternoon. Sue _____ him and Terry was angry. _____ said he was _____ up with the leisure centre. When _____ arrived at school, _____ walked away. I think he _____ Sue, but she teases him _____ the time. It's funny, because she likes him _____ .

## LANGUAGE WORK

# The past tense of 'to be' ▶2.1–2

**1** a Use the words to complete this table.

were   were not   was   wasn't   weren't   was not

| | | | |
|---|---|---|---|
| I | | | |
| He | ........ | | |
| She | ........ | ill | yesterday. |
| It | ... ... | | |
| | | busy | last week. |
| You | ........ | fed up | on Sunday. |
| We | ........ | | |
| They | ... ... | | |

b Make a statement and a question with each group of words.

**A** he/ill/was
**B** busy/you/were

c Now complete this rule with these two words.

verb   subject

> To make past tense questions with 'to be' we put the .......... in front of the .......... .

**2** Ask your partner about his/her weekend. Ask about morning, afternoon, and evening for Saturday and Sunday.

Example
**A** 'Where were you on Saturday morning?'
**B** 'I was at the swimming pool.'

18

# The past simple tense ▶2.3–4

 **3**  **a**  Complete this table.

| present | past | | present | past |
|---------|------|---|---------|------|
| play | ............. | | tease | ............. |
| help | ............. | | want | ............. |
| work | ............. | | paint | ............. |
| watch | ............. | | need | ............. |

**b**  Check the verbs in the Victoria Road story.

**c**  Complete this rule.

> To make the past simple tense of regular verbs
> we add .......... to the verb.

**d**  Read the past tenses aloud. How are
'wanted', 'painted', and 'needed'
different from the others?

**4**  Some verbs have an irregular past.

**a**  Find examples in the Victoria Road story.

**b**  Which of these verbs have an irregular past
form?

come   use   do   get   work   sit   run   sing
stand   stay   live   buy   make   leave   see

**5**  Complete the text. Put the verbs in brackets
into the past simple tense.

When I .............. (come) home from school last

Friday, I .............. (start) to feel ill, so I .............. (go)

to bed. The next morning I still ............. (feel) ill, so

Mum .............. (call) the doctor. He .............. (say)

that I .............. (have) flu. For the first few days I

.............. (stay) in bed. I .............. (sleep) most of the

time, but I also .............. (listen) to the radio and

.............. (read) some magazines. On Tuesday I

.............. (get up) and I .............. (watch) TV. In the

afternoon my friends .............. (arrive). They

.............. (tell) me all about school, and they

.............. (bring) me some videos. They ..............

(be) very good. But by Friday I .............. (be) bored

at home and I .............. (want) to go back to school.

# The past simple tense: negative ▶2.5

**6**  Look at these sentences.

I **played** table tennis yesterday.

I **didn't play** football yesterday.

**Complete this table with the correct parts of
the verbs in this list.**

watches   go   went   watched   watch   goes

| I He She It We You They | | didn't | ....... to the shop | yesterday. |
| | | | ....... television | on Sunday. |

**7**  Here are the things Sue wanted to do last
weekend. She didn't do all of them.

| THINGS TO DO | | | |
|---|---|---|---|
| | **Item** | | **Done** |
| 1 | Help in the shop | | ✓ |
| 2 | Wash hair | | |
| 3 | Phone Terry | | ✓ |
| 4 | Watch TV quiz show | | |
| 5 | Go to cinema | | ✓ |
| 6 | Iron clothes | | |
| 7 | Paint bedroom | | ✓ |
| 8 | Play on the computer | | ✓ |
| 9 | Stay in bed late on Sunday | | |
| 10 | Do homework | | ✓ |
| 11 | | | |

**a**  Say what Sue did and didn't do.

> Example
> *She helped in the shop.*
> *She didn't wash her hair.*

**b**  Say whether you did these things.

─────── optional activity ───────

**FOLLOW UP**

 **8**  Describe your weekend. Write five things
that you did and five things that you didn't
do.

19

# READING

**1** Look at the pictures. Who is the text about? Find his name in the text.

**2** Look at this list of places. Read the story quickly and put them in the correct order. Don't worry if you don't understand everything.

Mississippi     Sun Records recording studio
Memphis       Hollywood
Germany       Graceland
New York

# The King of Rock and Roll

Elvis Presley came from a very poor family. He was born on 8 January 1935 in Mississippi. Elvis loved music. He went to church every Sunday and sang in the choir. When he was 13, his mother bought him a guitar. In the same year Elvis and his family moved to Memphis, Tennessee.

One day in 1954 he went to a recording studio called Sun Records. He wanted to make a record for his mother's birthday. The secretary at the studio heard Elvis and she told her boss, Sam Phillips. Phillips became Elvis' manager and Elvis made his first single – *That's All Right, Mama*. When disc jockeys played it on their radio stations, American teenagers went wild. Many American parents didn't like Elvis. He was too sexy.

In 1955 Elvis appeared on TV in New York. The following year he went to Hollywood and made his first film *Love Me Tender*. In the next two years he had many hit records. Then in 1958 Elvis joined the American army and went to Germany. When he returned to the United States in the early 60s, pop music was not the same. British groups like The Beatles and The Rolling Stones were the new stars.

Elvis was a millionaire, but he was a very lonely man. In his last years he became fat and depressed. He died of a heart attack on 16 August 1977 in his mansion at Graceland, Memphis.

But for his millions of fans, Elvis is still the King. Shane Lyons has got more than 250 albums by Elvis and videos of all his films. 'Man, he was great,' says Shane. 'Elvis could really sing. Not like these kids today with all their electronic machines. He was the King, man, the King of Rock and Roll.'

**3** Read the text again. Choose the correct dates and match them to the places in Exercise 2.

| | | | |
|---|---|---|---|
| 1932 | 1977 | 1958 | 1935 |
| 1956 | 1955 | 1954 | 1980 |
| 1948 | 1951 | 1965 | 1974 |

**4** Read the text again. Write down what Elvis did at each place.

## WORD WORK

**5** Find all the irregular past tenses in the text.

— optional activity —

## FOLLOW UP

**6** Use the information from exercises 2, 3, and 4. Write a short biography of Elvis.

Example
*In 1935 Elvis Presley was born in Mississippi. In 1948…*

# LISTENING

**1** a  Listen to the tape. Who are the people speaking?

b Connect the names with the things.

| | |
|---|---|
| Jane Asquith | teddy bear |
| Shane Lyons | autograph |
| Johanne Palmer | holiday |

**2** a What can you remember about each fan?

b Which of these were mentioned?

| | | | |
|---|---|---|---|
| plate | statue | album | clock |
| poster | pen | radio | T-shirt |
| book | mirror | sweatshirt | teddy bear |
| bag | pencil | picture | video |

c Listen again and check your ideas.

**3** a Do you agree with Shane's ideas?

b What souvenirs do you collect of your favourite pop or sports stars?

─── optional activities ───

**4**  Listen and complete the song.

## Blue Suede Shoes

*Well, it's one for the ........! Two for the ........!*
*Three to get ........! Now go, cat, go!*
*But don't you step on my ......... Suede Shoes.*
*Well you can ..... anything, but lay off ..... Blue Suede Shoes.*

*Well you can knock me .........,*
*Step in my .........,*
*Slander my ........ all over the place*
*Do ........... that you want to do.*
*But oh, oh Honey, lay off of my ........*
*And don't you step on my ........ Suede Shoes.*
*You can ...... anything, but lay off of ..... Blue Suede Shoes.*

*Well, you can ........ my house,*
*Steal my .......,*
*........ my liquor from an old fruit jar.*
*You can do ........... that you want to do.*
*But oh, oh Honey, lay off of my ........*
*And don't you step on my ........ Suede Shoes.*
*You can ..... anything, but lay off of ..... Blue Suede Shoes.*

**Words and music by Carl Lee Perkins**

## FOLLOW UP

**5** Choose ten words from Exercise 2b. Write a sentence for each to show the meaning.

# INTERACTION

## The past simple tense: questions ▶2.5

**1** a Look at these sentences.

**Did** you **play** tennis yesterday?
Yes, I **played** tennis at the leisure centre.

**Did** you **go** to London last week?
Yes, I **went** to London on Tuesday.

b Now complete this rule.

> To make past tense questions, we use:
>
> ........... + subject + verb stem.

**2** Here are some facts about Elvis Presley's life. Write the questions.

Example
*Where was he born?*
He was born in Mississippi.

When .............................................. to Memphis?
They moved there in 1948.

Where ...................................... his first record?
He made it at Sun Records recording studio.

How old ....................................................... ?
He was 19.

When .................................................. the army?
In 1958.

Where ....................................................... ?
He went to Germany.

How ........................................................ ?
He died of a heart attack.

**3** Work in pairs. A DJ is interviewing a famous person about his/her life.

a Write down the questions the DJ will ask.

b **A** is the DJ. **B** is the star. Start like this:

*Today I'm interviewing ................................. .*

*Hello, ..................... . Where were you born?*

c Change roles and do another interview.

─── optional activity ───

## FOLLOW UP

**4** Write your interview from Exercise 3.

21

# GUIDED WRITING

## My favourite pop star

### Paragraphs

 **1** When we write a longer text we divide it up into paragraphs. Each paragraph has a topic.

**a** Look at the text on page 20. Match these topics to the correct paragraphs.

How did he become famous?
an evaluation
his career
his early life
his private life

**b** In which paragraph would you put this information?

He married Priscilla Beaulieu and they had a daughter called Lisa-Marie.
Elvis was Sam Phillips' dream.
You can still hear his records on radio stations all over the world.
Elvis wanted a bicycle but it was too expensive.
He also made a lot of films.

 **2** **Write about your favourite pop star.**

**a** Use the paragraph topics in Exercise 1a.

**b** Make notes for each paragraph.

**c** Write your paragraphs.

**Learning** *diary* **2**

What have you learnt in this unit?

**A** Do the self-check in the Workbook. Check any grammar problems in the reference section on pages 101–107.

**B** Have you used the reference material during this unit? What for? How did it help you?

**Complete your learning diary.**

▶ Pronunciation: page 97

# Main grammar point:
## The present continuous tense

*What are you doing?*

*We're mending Casey's bike.*

*Kamala isn't helping us. She's working in her parents' shop. She works there every weekend.*

## Learning objectives

| | |
|---|---|
| **Learning to learn:** | Recording new vocabulary |
| **Victoria Road:** | Describing what people are doing |
| **Language work:** | The present continuous tense ▶ 3.1–3<br>Comparing the present continuous and present simple tenses ▶ 3.4 |
| **Reading:** | Describing a town<br>Matching information in a map and texts |
| **Listening:** | Describe what's happening |
| **Interaction:** | Asking for and giving directions |
| **Project:** | Our town |

## Learning to learn: *Recording new vocabulary*

a How do you record vocabulary? Do you have a separate vocabulary book?

b Which of these ways do you use? Which do you think are the most useful?

- in alphabetical order
- by word class (nouns, adjectives, verbs, etc.)
- unit by unit
- by topics (sport, furniture, travel, etc.)
- with a translation

c What extra information can you put in your own vocabulary records?

Examples
*irregular forms (such as plurals), example sentences*

# *Jackie arrives*

**1** Look at the picture story.

  **a** Who are the new people?

  **b** Why are they in Victoria Road?

  **c** What does Terry think of the girl?

  **d** What does Terry do?

  **e** What do the others think?

**2** Listen and follow in your book.

**Terry**  Hi. What are you doing?

**Sue**  We're mending Casey's bike. You're up early, aren't you?

**Terry**  Why aren't you playing football today, Casey? You play football every Saturday, don't you?

**Casey**  I'm not playing this week. I've hurt my knee.

**Sue**  Oh, look. I think we're getting new neighbours. Some people are looking at old Mrs Boswell's house.

**Jackie**  Oh, why are we moving to this place? I want to stay in Manchester. All my friends are there.

**Mrs Wright**  You can make some new friends here, dear. Go and talk to those young people over there.

**Sue**  Oh, the girl isn't going into the house. She's crossing the road. I think she's coming over here.

**Jackie**  Hi, I'm Jackie – Jackie Wright.

**Terry**  (thinks) Mmmm. She's gorgeous.

**Sue**  Oh, hello. My name's Sue and thi…

**Terry**  Hi, I'm Terry. Are you moving into number 23?

**Jackie**  Well, we aren't moving in today, but my parents want to buy the house. Is there much to do round here?

**Vince**  Well, Terry doesn't like…

**Terry**  It's a great place. There's a cinema in town. And there are two good cafés and a park round the corner. And there's a really great leisure centre. I go there a lot.

**Jackie**  Are you doing anything at the moment?

**Sue**  Terry never does anything.

**Terry**  Well, er, actually I'm going to the shop. Do you want to come? I can show you around.

**Casey**  I don't believe it!

**Vince**  I think Terry's in love.

**Sue**  Hmph.

Mmmm. She's gorgeous.

Hi, I'm Jackie – Jackie Wright.

4

Are you doing anything at the moment?

Terry never does anything.

Well, er, actually I'm going to the shop. Do you want to come?

5

I don't believe it.

I think Terry's in love.

Hmph.

6

## Useful expressions

**5** How do you say these expressions in your language?

### You're up early.

### round the corner

### I don't believe it.

### Is there much to do round here?

### I can show you around.

### He's in love (with)...

### Are you doing anything at the moment?

**3** **Right, Wrong or Don't know?**

| | ✓ | ✗ | ? |
|---|---|---|---|
| **a** It's Saturday. | ☐ | ☐ | ☐ |
| **b** Jackie is from Manchester. | ☐ | ☐ | ☐ |
| **c** She wants to move to Victoria Road. | ☐ | ☐ | ☐ |
| **d** Jackie and her family are moving in today. | ☐ | ☐ | ☐ |
| **e** Vince doesn't like Jackie. | ☐ | ☐ | ☐ |
| **f** Terry says he doesn't like the place. | ☐ | ☐ | ☐ |

— optional activity —

**4** Close your book. Listen again.

**6** **a** Work in groups of four. One person is Terry, one is Sue, one is Jackie, and one is all the other parts.

**b** Read the dialogue.

— optional activity —

### FOLLOW UP

**7** Write a sentence about each picture in the story. Use these verbs.

cross    mend    talk    look    go
introduce herself

## The present continuous tense ▶3.1–3

 **a** **Look at this sentence.**

We're mend**ing** Casey's bike.

> This is the 'present continuous' tense. It
> describes what is happening now.

**Find more verbs like this in the Victoria
Road story.**

**b** **Complete this table.**

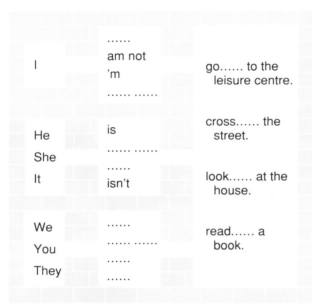

| I | ...... am not 'm ...... ...... | go...... to the leisure centre. |
| He She It | is ...... ...... isn't | cross...... the street. |
| We You They | ...... ...... ...... ...... ...... | look...... at the house. read...... a book. |

**c** **Make a statement and a question with each group of words.**

**A** the/crossing/Jackie/street/is
**B** they/house/at/looking/the/are

**d** **How do we make questions in the present continuous tense?**

## 2 How observant are you?

**a** Study the picture on page 27 for two minutes. Ask your teacher for any words you want.

**b**  Close your book. Listen and answer the questions.

**c** Look at the picture and check your answers.

**d** Ask your partner questions about the picture.

*Examples*
*How many adults are there?*
*What is the man in the kitchen doing?*

## The present continuous and present simple tenses ▶3.4

 **Look at these two sentences.**

Are you **doing** anything at the moment?
Terry never **does** anything.

**a** What tense is used in:
- the first sentence?
- the second sentence?

**b** Look at the Victoria Road story again and complete these sentences.

**1** You .......... football every Saturday.

**2** I .......... this week. I've hurt my knee.

**3** There's a great leisure centre. I ............ there a lot.

**4** .......... to the shop. Do you want to come?

**c** Complete this rule.

> We use the present continuous tense for
> something that is happening .......... .
> We use the present simple tense for
> something that happens ........................ .

 **Terry and Jackie are talking. Put these verbs into the correct tense.**

**a** We (go) to school at quarter to nine every day.

**b** What (do) your friends?
They (mend) Casey's bike.

**c** Casey (play) football every Saturday morning.

**d** Have you got any hobbies?
Yes, I (collect) stamps.

**e** What (do) your parents at the moment?
They (look) at the house.

**f** What (do) your father?
He (work) in an office.

**g** We (not move) in today.

**h** I (not do) anything at the moment.

**i** Kamala (work) in her parents' shop on Saturdays.

—— optional activity ——

**FOLLOW UP**

 **Look at your answers to Exercise 2b. Write the questions on the tape.**

# READING

**1** Look at the map of Hartfield. Below the map there are six texts. Only four of the texts are correct. Which are they?

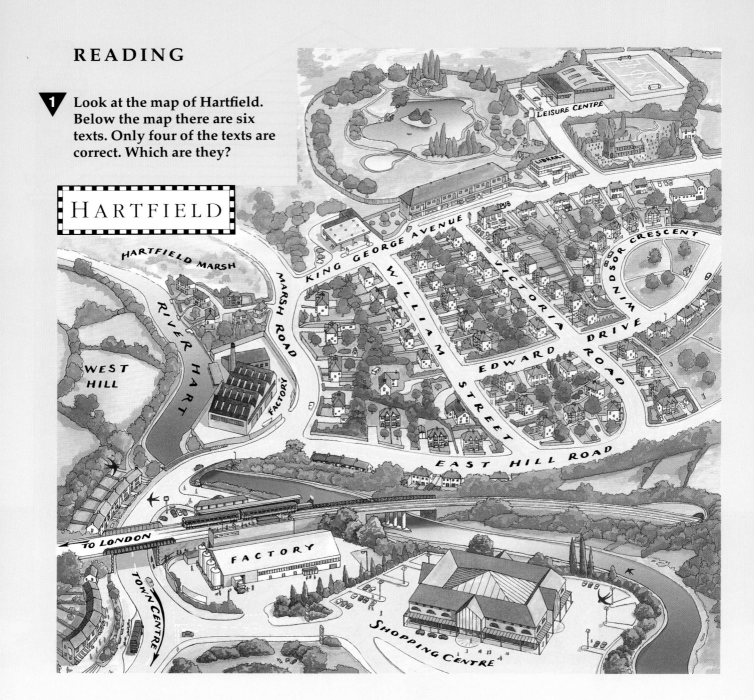

HARTFIELD

**A** Hartfield lies in a valley between two hills. The town gets its name from the River Hart. The name means a field on the River Hart. Today there are two bridges over the river. There is also a railway tunnel under the river.

**B** Many people from Hartfield work in offices in London. Sue's father travels up to London every day by train. But a lot of people work in Hartfield itself. There are two factories near the station and the town has a modern shopping centre.

**C** All the young people from Victoria Road go to Hartfield Secondary School. Terry and his friends go to school by bus. The bus stop is in King George Avenue in front of the library.

**D** There's a park near Victoria Road. There's a lake in the middle of the park. Next to the park there's a leisure centre with a football pitch. Casey plays football here every Saturday. The centre is behind the church near the entrance to the park.

**E** There are some shops in King George Avenue. On one side of the street there is a newsagent's, a cafe and a library. The cafe is called the Fat Cat. On the opposite side of the street there is a petrol station, a supermarket and a hairdresser's.

**F** At the end of Victoria Road there is a small parade of shops. Kamala's parents own the newsagent's. They sell newspapers and magazines, sweets and cigarettes. Kamala and her family live in a flat above the shop. On the corner of Victoria Road there is a pub called the Red Lion.

**2 a Find these things on the map.**

the bus stop     the Red Lion
the church       the lake
the station      the railway tunnel

**b Which of these are not on the map?**

| | | |
|---|---|---|
| a bridge | a river | a park |
| a hospital | a castle | a swimming pool |
| a railway line | a lake | the sea |
| a forest | an island | a hill |
| a bus station | a canal | a marsh |

## W O R D    W O R K

**3 a Find as many words as possible to complete this table.**

| buildings | man-made features | natural features |
|---|---|---|
| factory | park | hill |
| | | |

**b Use a dictionary. Find two or more words for each list.**

**c Which of these things are there in your neighbourhood?**

─────── optional activities ───────

**How good is your memory?**

a Look at the map for one minute.

b Follow these instructions.

  **A** Close your book.
  **B** Ask 'How many ........... are there on the map?'
  **A** Give the answer.

  Example
  **B** *How many bridges are there on the map?*
  **A** *There are three bridges.*

## F O L L O W   U P

Learn the words in your lists for Exercise 3.

## LISTENING

# *Moving day*

**1 Look at the picture.**

a What is happening today?

b Have you ever moved house? What was it like?

c What do people have to do when they move house? Write down some useful words.

  Examples
  *pack, box*

 **2**  **Listen. You will hear some dialogues from the moving day. What is happening in each one?**

  Example
  *1 Jackie is getting up.*

**3 a Answer these questions.**

1 What time did Jackie get up?

2 What did Jackie put in the box?

3 What did the men drop?

4 Who cried?

5 What did Mr Wright ask Jackie for?

6 What is Mrs Moore's first name?

7 What did Jackie say about the leisure centre?

**b Listen again and check your ideas.**

─────── optional activities ───────

**4 What do you think of Jackie? What kind of person do you think she is?**

## F O L L O W   U P

**5 Use your answers to Exercises 2 and 3. Describe the moving day. Start like this.**
*Jackie got up at five o'clock. She didn't want ...*

## INTERACTION

### Excuse me . . .

**1** a 📼 Look at the map on page 28. Listen and complete the dialogue.

> Excuse me. Can you tell me how to get to the library?

> Yes it's ............. King George Avenue. ............. down here. Take the ............. turning ............ the right.

> Second on the right?

> Yes, that's ............................. .
> The library is ........................... .

> On the left?

> Yes, there's a bus stop ............. it.

> Thank you.

b Where are the people on the map?

c Work in pairs. Role play your completed dialogue.

**2** Work in pairs. You are at the station. Make the dialogues for getting to:

- Edward Drive.
- the Hartfield leisure centre.

**3** You are outside your school. Someone asks you the way to these places.

- the bus station
- the town centre
- the police station
- the post office
- the hospital

**Make the conversations.**

—— optional activity ——

**FOLLOW UP**

**4** Write one of your dialogues from Exercise 3.

## PROJECT

### *Our town*

**1** A group of teenagers from another country is coming to visit your town. Make a project to introduce them to the town.

a Draw a map. Label the important places in the town.

b Write short texts about some of the places.

Examples
*your school     the local shops     places to go*

c Add some pictures of the town.

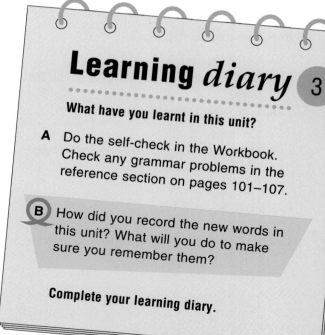

**Learning *diary*** 3

**What have you learnt in this unit?**

**A** Do the self-check in the Workbook. Check any grammar problems in the reference section on pages 101–107.

**B** How did you record the new words in this unit? What will you do to make sure you remember them?

**Complete your learning diary.**

# 4 revision

present simple
present continuous
past simple

 **1 Look at the tenses above.**

a For each tense write down two things that you know about:

positive statements
negative statements
questions
spelling rules
use

b Check your ideas in the Grammar reference.

 **2 Look at the newspaper article.**

a Who is it about?

b What did he do last Saturday?

c Why did he do it?

Actor Craig Barnes doesn't get up early on Saturdays. He works at the theatre on Friday night and he goes to bed very late, so he usually stays in bed on Saturday mornings. But last week he was up early. He took the bus to Covent Garden at half past eight and he went to a clothes shop. He was in the shop all day, but he didn't buy anything. He sold things.

Last Saturday shoppers in Covent Garden in London had an unusual day. For 12 hours over 300 stars from television, pop music, sport and the cinema worked in the shops, pubs, cafes and restaurants in Covent Garden. More than 100,000 customers came to see them.

 **3 Say whether Craig does or doesn't do these things on a normal Saturday morning.**

get up late
work in a shop
stay in bed
sell things
go to Covent Garden.

 **4 Here's the second part of the article. Put the verbs in brackets into the past tense.**

The idea ............ (be) simple. People ............ (come) to see the stars, they ............ (buy) things and the shop owners ............ (give) 5 per cent to charity. But the stars ............ only ............ (not sell) things. They also ............ (sign) autographs and ............ (kiss) their fans. Kisses ............ (cost) £5 each.

A young secretary, Joanne Walker, ............ (decide) to go to the hairdresser's and she ............ (see) a member of her favourite pop group. She ............(can't) believe her luck. In the sports shop next door the shop assistants ............ (be) all international footballers. In other shops customers ............ (meet) writers, a boxer, a TV cook, DJs and many others. Everyone ............ (have) a great time and at the end of the day more than £100,000 ............ (go) to charity.

 **5 a Make a chart like this.**

| jobs | places |
|------|--------|
|      |        |

b Read the two parts of the article again. Find as many words as possible for your chart.

c Can you add any more words?

**6 Look at the photograph. What are the people doing? Use these verbs.**

put    look at    take

**7** Here is part of an interview with another shopper. Use the cues to make the questions.

**Interviewer** (What time/arrive/at Covent Garden)

**Boy** At about eight o'clock.

**Interviewer** (come/by car)

**Boy** No, I came by bus.

**Interviewer** (get up/early/every Saturday)

**Boy** No, I usually stay in bed.

**Interviewer** (Why/be/here/today)

**Boy** A lot of stars are working in the shops.

**Interviewer** (wait/to see/anyone special)

**Boy** Yes, I'm waiting to see Sally Wallis, you know, the singer.

**Interviewer** (she/ work/in this shop)

**Boy** Yes, she is.

**Interviewer** (like/her)

**Boy** Oh, I think she's great.

──── optional activity ────

**FOLLOW UP**

 **Imagine you are organizing a charity event like this.**

**a** Discuss these questions.

Where will you hold the event?
Which famous personalities will you try to get?
What will the personalities do?

**b** Write a newspaper report about your event.

## listening skills
## question forms

**1**  Look at the pictures below.

**a** Who is the man?

**b** Why is he talking to the boy and the girl?

**2**  📼 Listen to the first part of the dialogue. Find out:

**a** Who are the boy and the girl?

**b** Where are they from?

**c** What are the questions about?

**3**  **a** What questions do you think the DJ will ask?

**b** Who do you want to win?

**4**  📼 Listen to the second part of the tape. Find out what happens.

**a** What questions did the DJ ask?

**b** What were the answers?

**c** Who got each question right?

**d** What was the score after the first round?

**5**  Listen again and check your answers.

You're listening to the Mike Moon show on Radio Hotline – everybody's favourite radio station. It's 3.30 and so it's time for the Hotline telephone quiz. Let's meet our two contestants.

──── optional activity ────

**FOLLOW UP**

 **Make your own Hotline telephone quiz.**

▶ Pronunciation: page 98

32

# Main grammar points:
## The future simple tense

*Sue won't be at home next week.*

*Oh, where will she be?*

*She'll be on holiday in Spain.*

## must, mustn't, needn't

*You must take your swimsuit, but you needn't take a coat. You mustn't forget your passport.*

### Learning objectives

**Learning to learn:** Working things out

**Victoria Road:** Talking about the future

**Language work:** The future simple: will ▶ 5.1 – 3

**Reading:** Using clues to predict what a text is about
Working out vocabulary from context
'If' clauses ▶ 5.4

**Listening:** Making arrangements
must, mustn't, needn't ▶ 5.5

**Interaction:** Using a timetable
Buying a train ticket

**Guided writing:** Summarising

## Ω Learning to learn: *Working things out*

a   When you learn a language, you can work out a lot of things for yourself. Look at the learning to learn activities in this unit. What must you work out in each one?.

b   As you work through the unit, make a note of things that you worked out for yourself.

# Sue goes to Spain

### 1 Look at the pictures.

a Who is Sue's letter from?

b What is it about?

c What does Jackie suggest?

d What is the telephone call about?

### 2  Listen and follow in your book.

**Sue** Listen to this. It's from Carmen. 'Would you like to come and stay with us next month?' Oh, Dad. Can I go, oh, please, please, can I, Dad, can I?

**Mr Scott** Where will you stay? It will be very hot in Madrid in August.

**Sue** We won't be in Madrid. We'll be at Carmen's uncle's house in the country. It's near the coast.

**Mrs Scott** But, how will you get there?

**Sue** I'll fly to Madrid. Carmen and her father will meet me at the airport and then we'll drive to the country. Oh, come on, please. I'll be all right.

**Mr Scott** Well, all right, then, but…

**Sue** Oh, thank you, Dad. I'll love you forever. Oh, it will be wonderful. Three weeks in Spain. I'll go swimming in the sea and sunbathe on the beach and I'll…Oh, I'm so excited.

#### Later

**Jackie** Shall we all go to the seaside next Sunday?

**Terry** Oh, yes, that's a great idea.

**Vince** Sue can't come. She'll be at the airport. She's going to Spain next Sunday.

**Jackie** Oh, what a pity.

**Have you got your passport, your tickets, your Spanish money and all your clothes?**

**Yes, Mum. Don't panic.**

4

**Aunt Ada is very ill. Your mum and I must go and see her.**

**Oh, Dad. How will I get to the airport? I can't carry all this luggage on my own.**

5

**Vince and Terry will help you, won't you, boys?**

6

### Saturday evening

**Mrs Scott** Have you got your passport, your tickets, your Spanish money and all your clothes?

**Sue** Yes, Mum. Don't panic.

**Mr Scott** I'm sorry, Sue, but I can't take you to the airport by car tomorrow. Aunt Ada is very ill. Your mum and I must go and see her.

**Sue** Oh, Dad. How will I get to the airport? I can't carry all this luggage on my own.

**Mr Scott** That's all right. You can go by train. Vince and Terry will help you, won't you, boys?

### What do you think? What will Vince and Terry do?

**3**

## Right, Wrong or Don't know?

| | | ✓ | ✗ | ? |
|---|---|---|---|---|
| **a** | Carmen wrote the letter in July. | ☐ | ☐ | ☐ |
| **b** | Sue will travel to Spain by plane. | ☐ | ☐ | ☐ |
| **c** | Carmen's parents will meet Sue at the airport. | ☐ | ☐ | ☐ |
| **d** | Sue will be in Spain for a month. | ☐ | ☐ | ☐ |
| **e** | Jackie wants to go to London next Sunday. | ☐ | ☐ | ☐ |
| **f** | Casey will go with Jackie. | ☐ | ☐ | ☐ |
| **g** | Sue must take a taxi to the airport. | ☐ | ☐ | ☐ |

—— optional activity ——

**4**

### Close your book. Listen again.

## Useful expressions

**5** How do you say these expressions in your language?

**How will I get to . . . ?**

**Don't panic.**

**in the country**

**I'm so excited.**

**Oh, what a pity.**

**Would you like to . . . ?**

**on my own**

**6** a Work in groups of three. One person is Sue and Jackie, one is Mr Scott and Terry, and one is Mrs Scott and Vince.

b Role play the dialogue.

── optional activity ──

**FOLLOW UP**

**7** Complete Carmen's letter.

5th July

Dear Sue

Hi. How ............ you? It's very hot ............ Spain now. Would you ............ to come and stay with us next ............ ? We ............ be in Madrid. We'll be ............ my uncle's house in the ............... . If you ............ to Madrid, my ............ and I will ............ you ............ the airport and then ............ drive ............ the country. We'll be at my ............ house for three ............ . My uncle's house ............ near the ............ so we can go ............... every day and we can ............ on the beach. I hope you ............ come... .

## LANGUAGE WORK

# The future simple tense: will ▶5.1–3

**1** a Complete this table with the short forms.

| I | | go to the seaside | |
|---|---|---|---|
| He | will | catch the 7.15 | |
| She | ...... | train | tomorrow. |
| It | | be late | |
| We | will not | have a great time | next week. |
| You | ...... | fly to Greece | |
| They | | | |

We call this the future simple.

b Complete this rule.

> To make the future simple we put ........... or
> ........... in front of the verb. For the negative
> we put ........... ........... or ........... in front of
> the verb.

**Note:** With 'I' and 'we' we can also say 'shall/shan't', especially in questions. Find an example in the story.

c What is the short form of 'shall'?

**2** Look at this list of things. What do you think Sue will or won't do on her holiday in Spain?

Example
*She will meet Carmen's family.*
*She won't go to school.*

| | |
|---|---|
| meet Carmen's family | eat English food |
| go to school | write some postcards |
| swim in the sea | do her homework |
| sunbathe on the beach | feel homesick |
| make new friends | go to a disco |
| learn Spanish | go skiing |
| stay in Madrid | work on the farm |

 **3** a Put these words in the correct order to make questions in the future simple.

   A  stay/where/you/will

   B  right/will/he/all/be

b  Complete this rule.

> To make questions in the future simple we put
> will ............................. the subject.

 **4** Look at the story on page 34 again. Here are Sue's answers. What were the questions?

Example
*How will you travel to Spain?*
*By plane.*

a  How ........................................................?
   I'll get the train.

b  How ........................................................?
   Vince and Terry will help me.

c  Where ......................................................?
   At Carmen's uncle's house in the country.

d  How long ..................................................?
   Three weeks.

e  What ........................................................?
   I'll sunbathe on the beach and visit lots of places.
   I'll have a great time.

─── optional activity ───

**FOLLOW UP**

 **5** What will you do next weekend? Write six sentences about what you will do. Write six questions to ask your friend what he/she will do.

Examples
I'll tidy my room.      Will you tidy your room?
I'll help my dad.       Will you ...?

**THINGS TO DO**

☐ Tidy room

☐ Help Dad

☐ Wash car

# READING

**1 a** **Before you read the text, check the meaning of these words:**

team        the Earth        vehicle
continent        expedition

**b** **Look at the words above and the pictures. What do you think the text is about?**

**2** **Read the text.**

**a** Match the words in Exercise 1a to the correct paragraphs.

**b** Read again. What does the text say about each of the things?

## An expedition to save the planet

Next spring an international expedition will set out on a very important journey around the world. For 13 months Mark Hiley and the four other members of the expedition will study and report on the environment.

The expedition will visit every continent except Antarctica. From Europe the team will drive south into Africa, then east to Asia and Australasia. From here they will travel north again to Japan before they cross the Pacific Ocean to South America. Then they will travel to North America and across the Atlantic Ocean to London.

There will be three teams of five people. They will include doctors, mechanics, scientists and photographers. Only one team will travel round the world. The other teams will provide help and support. If a member of the first team is ill, for example, someone from another team will fly out to replace them.

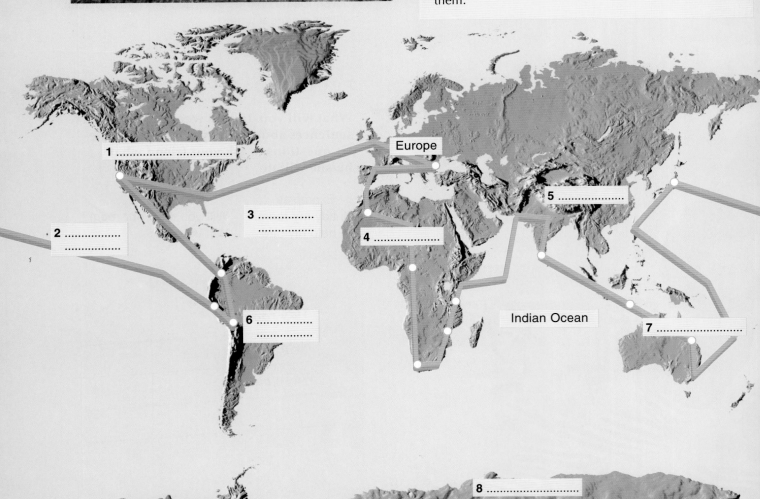

1 .................................

2 .................................

3 .................................

4 .....................

5 .....................

6 .................

7 .........................

8 ..........................

Europe

Indian Ocean

They will use two special vehicles. They will go to some difficult and dangerous places, and they will be on the road in spring, summer, autumn and winter. So they will need a lot of extra equipment. Each vehicle will cost £120,000.

The expedition will be on television all over the world and it will also be on the internet. 'That's important,' says Henrietta Boyd, the scientific officer. 'We want to show people what is really happening to the world. We are doing terrible things to the Earth and if we don't change, we'll destroy it. If people see the problems, they will try to help.'

 **3  Answer these questions.**

a  When will the expedition start?

b  How many continents will they visit?

c  Who will lead the expedition?

d  Why will they need three teams?

e  Why will the vehicles be so expensive?

f  How will people find out about the expedition?

 **4  Write the missing names of the continents and oceans on the map.**

| W | O | R | D |   | W | O | R | K |
|---|---|---|---|---|---|---|---|---|

 **5  Complete the lists:**

the four seasons: *spring* ......., ......., .......

the four points of the compass: *north*, ......., .......,

.......

the seven continents: *Africa*, ......., ......., ......., .......,

......., .......

## 'if' clauses ▶5.4

 **6  a  Complete this sentence from the text.**

If people ............. the problems, they ............. to help.'

b  **What tense is used in:**

The 'If' clause?   The main clause?

c  **Translate the sentence into your own language. What differences are there?**

d  **We call this kind of sentence a first conditional. Find more examples in the text.**

e  **Mark Hiley is answering questions at a news conference. Complete the sentences with the verbs in brackets.**

1  **Reporter** ............. you ............. the expedition if someone ............. ill? (stop/be)

**Mark Hiley** No, if someone ............. ill, the team doctor ............. to help. (be/try) If the person ............. to go to hospital, a member of another team .............. . (need/ fly out)

2  **Reporter** ............. you ............. next spring if you ............. enough money? (leave/not have got)

**Mark Hiley** No, if we ............. more money, we ............. a few months. (need/wait)

3  **Reporter** What ............. you ............. , if you ............. problems with the vehicles? (do/have)

**Mark Hiley** If it ............. a small problem, our mechanic ............. the vehicle. (be/mend) But if we ............. an important part, the support team ............. it to us. (want/send)

 **7  What do you think?**

a  What things will they need on the expedition?

b  What things do you think they will study?

c  Would you like to go on the expedition? Give your reasons.

### FOLLOW UP

 **8  Write an advertisement for people to join the expedition.**

a  Your advertisement should say:

What is Expedition Earth?
Where will it go?
How will the team travel?
What kind of people do you need?
Where should people write to?

b  Start like this:

*Do you want to see the world? Join us on Expedition Earth.*

# LISTENING

## *A day at the seaside*

**1**  **Listen to the conversation.**

**a** Where are Terry and Jackie going?

**b** How will they travel?

**c** What time must they meet?

**d** What will Jackie do later today?

**2** **Listen again and complete the conversation.**

**Terry** Vince and the others can't come.

**Jackie** So it will be just ..............

and ............., Terry.

**Terry** What time ........ we meet?

**Jackie** The train goes at a

.............. past ............ . I'll ...... the tickets today. Then we needn't be

........ the station too early.

**Terry** ....... ......... will it cost?

**Jackie** The fare will be ...... return. You needn't come to the station. If

you ...... me the money, I'll get the

............. .

**Terry** OK. So we ....... be at the

station by ....... past eight.

**Jackie** Yes. And remember I'll .......

your ticket. So, you mustn't .... late.

**Terry** Don't panic, Jack. I'll ....

there. What time will we get ........?

**Jackie** The ....... train is at half past

six. So we ............. miss it. Oh, it'll

be .......... . We'll ............... on the beach .

**Terry** We'll go .... the fun fair. And

we'll hire a ........ and go sailing on the boating lake. We'll ....... a really

good ....... .

## must, mustn't, needn't ▶5.5

**3** **a** Find the sentences with these words.

must   mustn't   needn't

**b** Translate the sentences into your own language. Do you notice any differences? What do you notice about the meaning of 'must' and 'mustn't' in English?

**c** Complete these sentences with 'must', 'mustn't' or 'needn't'.

1 Terry ............. give Jackie £9 for the fare.

2 They ............. be at the station by 7.30.

3 Terry ............ go and get his ticket.

4 They ............ miss the last train back.

5 Jackie ............. get Terry's ticket.

6 She ............ get tickets for Vince and the others.

7 Terry ............ get up late.

8 Jackie ............. forget to bring the tickets tomorrow.

─── optional activities ───

We'll have a really good time.

**4** The day at the seaside wasn't so great. Look at the pictures of the places on page 40. What do you think will happen?

**a** Write down your ideas.

Example
*Jackie will lose the tickets.*

**b** Work in pairs. Compare your answers with your partner.

**c**  Listen. What happened at the seaside? Were you right?

## FOLLOW UP

**5** Describe Terry and Jackie's day at the seaside.

Example
*Terry and Jackie bought their tickets the day before.*
*They wanted to get the 8.15 train but . . .*

## INTERACTION

# At the station

**1**  Listen to the dialogue at the railway station.

**2** **a** Complete the passenger's part of the dialogue.

**Passenger** .................. .

**Ticket clerk** Single or return?

**Passenger** .................. .

**Ticket clerk** That will be £18.

**Passenger** What time ....................in London?

**Ticket clerk** If you get the 10.54 train, you'll get to London at 14.14.

**Passenger** .................. .

**b** Listen again and check your answers.

─── optional activity ───

**3** Work in pairs. Role play your dialogue with your partner.

**4** Make dialogues for these situations. Use the timetable. You are in Lancaster.

| Lancaster ⟹ London | | | |
|---|---|---|---|
| **Mondays to Saturdays** | | **Sundays** | |
| Lancaster depart | London arrive | Lancaster depart | London arrive |
| 0625 **sx** | 0945 | 1509 | 1849 |
| 0625 **so** | 0945 | 1624 | 2014 |
| 0707 | 1016 | 1658 | 2044 |
| 0805 | 1135 | 1701 | 2044 |
| 0855 | 1204 | 1708 | 2103 |
| 0938 **sx** | 1244 | 1806 | 2206 |
| 0948 **so** | 1244 | 1942 | 2311 |
| 1054 | 1414 | 2258 | 0448 |
| 1154 | 1437 | | |
| 1221 | 1635 | | |
| 1422 | 1748 | | |
| 1625 | 1923 | | |
| 1636 | 2011 | **so** Saturday only | |
| 1725 | 2130 | **sx** except Saturday | |

**a** You want to travel to London with two friends. You must be there by 9 p.m.

**b** You want to travel to London. You needn't be there till 5 p.m.

**c** You want to travel to London. You must meet someone at 12 o'clock. You mustn't be late.

**d** You want to travel to London with a friend. You must be there by 2 o'clock on Saturday.

─── optional activity ───

## FOLLOW UP

**5** Write two of your dialogues from Exercise 4.

# GUIDED WRITING

## Summarising

**1** When you write a summary of a text you only give the most important information. A simple way to do this is to ask questions about the text. The summary should answer the questions.

**a** Look at the text on page 38. Match these question words to the correct paragraphs. (Note: two words go with one of the paragraphs.)

Who?  What?  Where?  When?  Why?  How?

**b** Here is part of the summary. It has the answers to the questions for paragraphs 1 and 2. Complete it with the answers for paragraphs 3–5.

> An international expedition will travel round the world to study the environment. The expedition will visit every continent except Antarctica. .......

# *The school trip*

**2** **a** Read this information. Match question words to the paragraphs.

**b** Write a summary to answer your questions.

**Here is some information about next year's school trip to France. The trip will take place 11–20 June.**

As usual we will spend the first three days in Paris. We'll have a sightseeing tour of the city and we'll also visit some of the famous places like the Eiffel Tower and the Louvre. From Paris we'll travel down to the South of France near Marseilles. We'll spend five days there.

Last year we went by coach, but we found that the journey was too long and we didn't have enough time to do everything. So this year we will go by train. I will provide more information about times later.

There will be places for 80 students on the trip. We will travel in two groups and there will be four teachers with each group. Mr Jacks, Mrs Clark, Mr Hudson and myself will go with Group 1. Mr and Mrs Peters, Mr Wall and Mrs Pink will go with Group 2.

I hope that everyone on the trip will have a good time, but please remember that it is an educational visit not a holiday. There will be some time for swimming and other sports, but we are going to France to study French culture and to use the French language as much as possible.

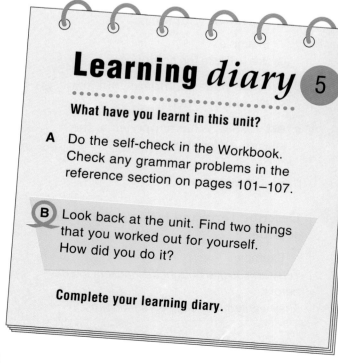

# Learning *diary* 5

What have you learnt in this unit?

**A** Do the self-check in the Workbook. Check any grammar problems in the reference section on pages 101–107.

**B** Look back at the unit. Find two things that you worked out for yourself. How did you do it?

**Complete your learning diary.**

▶ Pronunciation: page 98

# Main grammar point:
## The past continuous tense

*What were you doing when Terry and Jackie came into the shop?*

*I was putting things on the shelves.*

## Learning objectives

**Learning to learn:** Attitudes

**Victoria Road:** Telling a story

**Language work:** The past continuous tense ▶ 6.1–2

**Reading:** Using clues to put paragraphs in order
Making predictions
Comparing the past continuous and past simple tenses ▶ 6.3

**Listening:** Listening and organizing material

**Interaction:** Talking about an event in your life

**Guided writing:** Linking sentences

## ◯ Learning to learn: *Attitudes*

a   Look at this list of things in *New Hotline*. Can you add any more?

Victoria Road   role play   games   projects   grammar rules
listening   Learning to learn

b   Make a chart like this:

| I like these | I don't like these | I learn most from these |
|---|---|---|
|  |  |  |

c   Discuss your choices

# Kamala's story

**Hi, Sue. Did you have a good time in Spain?**

**I had a wonderful time. How are things here?**

**Well, all right, but...**

1

**Jackie and Terry came into our shop last Saturday. I was putting some things on the shelves. So they didn't see me.**

2

**While Dad wasn't looking, Terry picked up some packets of cigarettes and put them in his pocket.**

**No! Was he stealing them?**

3

## 1 Look at the picture story.

a Who is telling the story in pictures 2-5?

b When did it happen?

c What was Terry doing? Look at picture 6 for the word.

## 2 Complete the sentences with the correct names.

a ............. tells ............. about Terry.

b When ............. and ............. came into the shop, ............. was putting things on the shelves.

c While ............. was talking to .............,
............. tried to steal some cigarettes.

d As ............. was stealing them, he saw
............. .

e ............. put the cigarettes back.

f ............. is upset when she hears .............'s story. She thinks ............. was stealing the cigarettes for ............. .

## 3 🔲 Listen and follow in your book.

**Kamala** Hi, Sue. Did you have a good time in Spain?

**Sue** It was great! I had a wonderful time. How are things here?

**Kamala** Well, all right, but...

**Sue** But what?

**Kamala** Well, it's Terry.

**Sue** Huh! Don't talk to me about him. He didn't come to the airport with me. He went to the seaside with that Jackie.

**Kamala** That's the problem – Jackie. Jackie and Terry came into our shop last Saturday. I was putting some things on the shelves, so they didn't see me. Well, they were in the shop for a long time.

**Sue** What were they doing?

**Kamala** They weren't really doing anything. Jackie was reading the magazines and Terry was looking at the cigarettes.

**Sue** Cigarettes? Terry doesn't smoke.

**Kamala** No, but you know who does.

**Sue** Go on, what happened?

## What do you think?

**a** Why was Terry stealing cigarettes?

**b** How does Sue feel?

**c** What can Kamala and Sue do?

**Kamala** After about ten minutes, Jackie asked my father for something. While Dad wasn't looking, Terry picked up some packets of cigarettes and put them in his pocket.

**Sue** No! Was he stealing them?

**Kamala** Yes and no. You see, as he was taking them, he saw me.

**Sue** What did he do?

**Kamala** When he saw me, he went bright red. He put the cigarettes back and then they both left the shop.

**Sue** Oh, I don't believe it. Terry was shoplifting – and for her, too. Well, it serves him right.

**Kamala** Do you really mean that, Sue?

**Sue** No, Kam, I don't. Oh, poor Terry. He's such an idiot.

**4** **Right, Wrong or Don't know?**

| | ✓ | ✗ | ? |
|---|---|---|---|
| **a** Sue got back from Spain last night. | ☐ | ☐ | ☐ |
| **b** Terry went to the airport with Sue. | ☐ | ☐ | ☐ |
| **c** Kamala wasn't working in the shop when Jackie and Terry came in. | ☐ | ☐ | ☐ |
| **d** Jackie smokes. | ☐ | ☐ | ☐ |
| **e** Terry picked up three packets of cigarettes. | ☐ | ☐ | ☐ |
| **f** Terry left the shop on his own. | ☐ | ☐ | ☐ |
| **g** Kamala told her father that Terry was shoplifting. | ☐ | ☐ | ☐ |

— optional activity —

**5** **Close your book. Listen again.**

## Useful expressions

 **6** How do you say these expressions in your language?

> Don't talk to me about...
>
> How are things here?
>
> He went bright red.
>
> You know who...
>
> It serves him right.
>
> He's such an idiot.
>
> Do you really mean that?

 **7** a Work in pairs. Each person takes one of the parts.

b Role play the dialogue.

---
*optional activity*

### FOLLOW UP

 **8** Complete Kamala's diary.

**Saturday**

Terry and Jackie ............. into our shop today. I was ............. some things on the shelves. So they didn't ............. me. They were in the shop ............. a long time, but they ............. really doing anything. Jackie ............. reading the ............. and Terry was looking ............. the cigarettes. That was strange, because Terry ............. smoke. After about ten ............. , Jackie asked my father ............. something. While he was talking to Jackie, Terry picked ............. some packets of ............. . As he was ............. them in his ............., he ............. me. He went ............. red and he ............. the cigarettes back. Then they both ............. . I couldn't ............. it. Terry was ............. . He ............. ............. cigarettes ............. Jackie. What ............. I do?

---

## LANGUAGE WORK

# The past continuous tense

▶6.1–2

 **1** a Look at this sentence.

> I **was** putt**ing** some things on the shelves.

We call this the past continuous tense. It describes a continuous activity in the past. Find more sentences like this in the story.

b Complete this table.

| I | was | reading a book. |
|---|---|---|
| He | | look...... in a shop |
| She | ...... ...... | window. |
| It | wasn't | |
| | | watch...... television. |
| We | ...... | put...... something on the shelf. |
| You | were not | cross...... the street |
| They | ...... | writ...... a letter. |

c Complete these sentences about the Victoria Road story. Put the verbs in brackets into the past continuous tense.

1 Sue and Kamala ............. in a cafe. (sit)

2 They ............. a cup of coffee. (have)

3 Sue ............. a T-shirt from Spain. (wear)

4 Kamala ............. a T-shirt. (not wear)

5 They ............. about Sue's holiday. (not talk)

6 Kamala ............. Sue about Terry and Jackie. (tell)

 **2** Test your memory.

a Work in pairs. Look at the picture on page 27 for one minute.

b Close the book. What were the people in the picture doing? Write down everything you can remember.

Example
*A man was washing up in the kitchen.*

c Compare your list with another pair's. Who remembered the most activities?

# The past continuous tense: questions ▶6.2

▶6.2

**3** **a** Make a statement and a question with each group of words.

   **A** cigarettes/the/was/stealing/he
   **B** magazines/reading/they/were/the

**b** Complete this rule.

> To make questions in the past continuous
> tense we put ........... or ........... in front
> of the subject.

**4** Make Sue's questions to complete the dialogue. Use the cues provided.

Example
**Sue** *What were you doing?*
(What/you/do)

**Kamala** I was putting things on the shelves.

**Sue** Tell me about it again, Kamala.

............................................................?
(What/you/do)

**Kamala** I was putting things on the shelves.

**Sue** ............................................................?
(What/Jackie and Terry/do/in the shop)

**Kamala** They weren't really doing anything.

**Sue** ............................................................?
(What/Jackie/read)

**Kamala** A magazine.

**Sue** ............................................................?
(What/Terry/look at)

**Kamala** The cigarettes.

**Sue** ............................................................?
(What/your parents/do)

**Kamala** My mum wasn't in the shop and my dad was serving.

**Sue** ............................................................?
(What/Jackie and your father/talk about)

**Kamala** Jackie was asking him for something.

**Sue** ............................................................?
(Why/Terry/steal/the cigarettes)

**Kamala** I don't know, Sue.

**5** **a** What were you doing at these times?

   8 o'clock last night       on Wednesday evening
   an hour ago             when the lesson started
   at 6.30 this morning     in your earliest memory
   last Saturday afternoon

**b** Ask your partner what he/she was doing at these times.

   Example
   **A** *What were you doing at 8 o'clock last night?*
   **B** *I was .....*

— optional activity —

### FOLLOW UP

**6** Complete these questions and answers about the picture on page 27. Use these verbs.

eat  carry  watch  sit  play  iron  wear

   Example
*What was the boy on the bicycle wearing?*
*He was wearing red trousers.*

**a** What ................................................ ?
   He .......................................... red trousers.

**b** What ................................................ ?
   They .................................... Black Beauty.

**c** Where ................................................ ?
   It ..................................... under the table.

**d** What ................................................ ?
   They .......................................... a settee.

**e** What ................................................ ?
   It ............................................. a bone.

**f** Where ................................................ ?
   He ...................................... in the garden.

**g** What ................................................ ?
   She ........................................... a shirt.

## READING

**1** Look at these paragraphs. They are parts of a story, but they are in the wrong order. First look quickly through the paragraphs.

a  Who is the story about?

b  Where did it happen?

c  What happened to her?

d  Who did she meet?

**2** Read the paragraphs. Put them in the correct order. (Note: the end of the story is missing.)

# The adventure

**A** Just as I was sitting down, I saw Javier. He was running along behind the bus and waving to me. He was saying something, but I couldn't hear over the noise of the bus. Then the bus speeded up and I couldn't see Javier any more.

**B** I got off the bus at the bus station and walked to the shops. It took nearly two hours to get everything. While I was looking for the last few things, somebody called me. It was Carmen's friend, Javier.

**C** The bus didn't stop for quite a long time, but finally it stopped and I got off. I waited till the bus left and started to cross the street. Then I saw that it was a one-way street. There wasn't a bus stop on the other side. I didn't know anybody there and it was getting dark. What could I do?

**D** I finished my shopping and then we went somewhere for a cup of coffee. We had a long chat. Javier's very nice. And he speaks very good English. We talked for about an hour and then we walked to the bus station together.

**E** After about a quarter of an hour, however, I realized why Javier was chasing the bus. I was on the wrong bus and I didn't know where we were going! So I thought: 'I'll get off at the next bus stop. Then I'll cross the street and get the bus in the opposite direction back to the bus station.'

**F** When we got to the bus station, the bus was already there. It was just leaving, so I quickly said goodbye to Javier and ran for the bus. I got on just in time and the bus left. I found a seat at the back of the bus.

**G** When I got up today, everybody was busy. One of the neighbours was having a party in the evening, and Carmen's aunt and uncle were helping to get things ready. Carmen and I helped in the morning, too, but in the afternoon there was nothing for us to do, so I went into town and bought some souvenirs. I went on my own on the bus, because Carmen was visiting someone in the village.

**3** a  **How did you decide the order? What clues did you use?**

b  🎧 **Listen and check your order.**

48

— optional activity —

**4** **Read the story again. Answer these questions.**

a Why did Sue go to town?

b Why did she go on her own?

c Where did Sue get off the bus?

d How long was she in town?

e How did Sue know Javier?

f What did Sue and Javier do?

g Why was Javier chasing the bus?

h What did Sue plan to do when she got off the bus?

i Why couldn't she get back to the bus station?

**W O R D   W O R K**

**5**
a **Find all the words in the story connected with movement.**

b **Find the missing words from this table in the story.**

| | | somewhere |
|---|---|---|
| …………… | …………… | everywhere |
| …………… | anything | anywhere |
| nobody | …………… | nowhere |

# The past continuous and the past simple ▶6.3

**6**
a **Complete this sentence from Sue's story.**

While I …………… for the last few things,

somebody …………… me.

**What tenses are the two verbs in?**

b **Look at the difference.**

*I was looking for the last few things*
a continuous activity

*somebody called me*
a completed activity

c **Complete this rule.**

> We use the 'past continuous' for a …………… activity.
> We use the 'past simple' for a …………… activity.

d **Now complete this sentence.**

I …………… my shopping and then we

…………… somewhere for a cup of coffee.

**Why are both verbs in the past simple tense? Look at your rule in 'c'.**

e **Complete what Javier says. Use the verbs in brackets.**

As I …………… (come) home yesterday, I

…………… (meet) Carmen's friend, Sue. She

…………… (look) in a shop window when I

…………… (see) her. We …………… (go) for a

cup of coffee and we …………… (have) a chat.

Then we …………… (walk) to the bus station.

Sue's bus …………… just …………… (leave)

when we …………… (arrive) at the bus station, so

Sue …………… (say) goodbye quickly and

…………… (run) to the bus. As she ……………

(get) on, I …………… (realize) it was the wrong

bus. I …………… (run) after the bus, but it

…………… (travel) too fast.

**7** **What do you think?**

a What could Sue do? List some ideas.

b How does the story end? Make an ending.

c 📼 Listen. You will hear the end of the story. Compare it with your own ending.

— optional activity —

**FOLLOW UP**

**8** Listen to the end of the story again. Make notes then write the last paragraph of the story.

# LISTENING

## The cat

**1** Look at the pictures.

   **a** Who is in each picture?

   **b** Where are they?

   **c** What are they doing?

**2** Use the pictures to make a story.

**3** ▣ Listen to the dialogue on the tape.

   **a** Put the pictures in the correct order.

   **b** Compare this order with your own ideas.

**4** Match these verbs to the correct pictures in the story of the cat.

look  refuse  hurt  scream  stand  fall off
crash  fetch  stroke  run  cry  climb down
get into  sit  drive away  shout  land  get
grab  climb up  arrive  wear  scratch

**A**

**B**

**C**

**D**

**E**

**F**

**G**

## FOLLOW UP

 **5** **Use the verbs in Exercise 4. Complete this story of the cat.**

On Saturday the Robinsons visited Peter and Carol's grandmother. When they ......................., the old lady .......................... in the garden. She .......................... up into a tree and she .......................... . Her cat, Timmy, was in a big tree and she couldn't get him down.

Mr Robinson .......................... a ladder. Carol .......................... to go up, because she .......................... her new dress. Peter didn't want to rescue the cat either, but his parents insisted. So Peter .......................... the ladder.

Peter .......................... the cat easily, but as he .........................., the cat .......................... his face. Poor Peter .......................... the ladder. Luckily he .......................... on the car, but he .......................... his arm. The cat .......................... under the car.

Peter's parents decided to take him to the hospital. So they all .......................... the car. But as they .........................., Carol .......................... 'Stop! The cat's under the car.' She .......................... Peter's arm and he .......................... . Mr Robinson was so surprised that he .......................... into the gate.

At the hospital all the Robinsons needed to see the doctor. Meanwhile Timmy was at home. He .......................... on Grandma's knee. She .......................... his head.

# INTERACTION

**1** **Read this story.**

## My accident

I've got a scar on my forehead. I got it when I was seven years old. I was standing on a stool to put some books on a shelf when I fell off. I hit my head on the corner of a cupboard. An ambulance took me to hospital. I needed eight stitches in the cut, but I was all right.

**2** **Everyone has an accident at some time in their life. Work in groups. Prepare questions to ask people about their accidents.**

   Example
   *How old were you?*
   *What were you doing?*
   *What did you do when . . . ?*

**Look at the story above for ideas.**

**3** **Find two people in the class and ask them about their accidents. Try to find out as much as possible.**

**4** **Tell the group what you have found out.**

## FOLLOW UP

**5** **Write the story of one of your accidents.**

# GUIDED WRITING

## Linking sentences

 **1** **a Look at these sentences about 'The adventure' on page 48.**

I got up today.

Everybody was busy.

One of the neighbours was having a party in the evening.

Carmen's aunt and uncle were helping to get things ready.

Carmen and I helped in the morning, too.

In the afternoon there was nothing for us to do.

I went into town.

I bought some souvenirs.

I went on my own on the bus.

Carmen was visiting someone in the village.

**b We can build these sentences into a paragraph. Look at paragraph G on page 48. How have the sentences been joined?**

 **2** **a We can build sentences into paragraphs in two ways.**

- We can use linking words (*when*, *and*, etc.).
- When two verbs are in the same tense and have the same subject, we can leave out the second subject.

**b Look at page 48 again. Find examples of these two ways of joining sentences.**

**c Use these ways of linking sentences when you write your own story.**

## *I don't believe it!*

 **3** **Write a funny or amazing story.**

**a** Think of a story. It can be true or imaginary.

**b** Write your story. Don't tell anyone if your story is true or not.

**c** Read other people's stories. Ask the writer some questions. Say whether you believe the story or not.

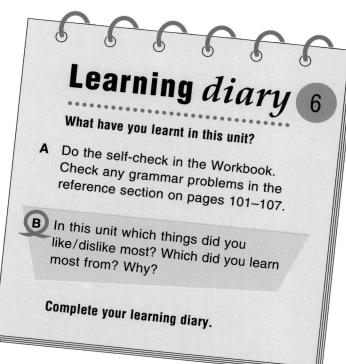

### Learning *diary* 6

**What have you learnt in this unit?**

**A** Do the self-check in the Workbook. Check any grammar problems in the reference section on pages 101–107.

**B** In this unit which things did you like/dislike most? Which did you learn most from? Why?

**Complete your learning diary.**

▶ Pronunciation: page 98

# Main grammar point:
## Comparing

*John's taller than me. He's the tallest boy in our class.*

SHOWROOM

*The red car is more expensive than the green one.*

*The white car is the most expensive.*

## Learning objectives

| | |
|---|---|
| **Learning to learn:** | Working in groups |
| **Victoria Road:** | Comparing people and things |
| **Language work:** | Comparatives and superlatives ▶ 7.1 |
| **Reading:** | Reading for main information<br>Describing clothes and fashions ▶ 7.2 |
| **Listening:** | Listening and matching conversations to places<br>a pair of ▶ 7.2 |
| **Interaction:** | Talking about clothes<br>Sizes |
| **Project:** | Oral presentations |

*comparisons*

**7**

## Learning to learn: *Working in groups*

**a**  Make a chart like this. Add some more ideas.

| Working in groups ||
|---|---|
| Positive | Negative |
| We can do bigger tasks like projects | I can work faster on my own |

**b**  What can you do about the negative points? Make a list of suggestions.

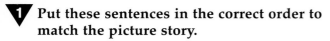

# Sue fights back

**1** **Put these sentences in the correct order to match the picture story.**

a Kamala shows Sue a magazine article.

b Terry borrows some money from Sue.

c Sue goes to buy some new clothes.

d Kamala and Sue see Jackie and Terry in the park.

e Jackie wants to leave the disco.

**2** **Look at the picture story again.**

a Why does Sue go to buy some new clothes?

b Does it work?

> I don't know what he sees in that Jackie. You're much better than her, Sue.

**TAKE a good look IN THE MIRROR**

Can you be more attractive?
Do you wear the best clothes for your figure?
Do you look after your hair?
Do you need new makeup?

> Have a look at this article in this magazine.

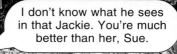

> Can I borrow it?

**①**

**②**

**3** 📼 **Listen and follow in your book.**

**Kamala** Doesn't it make you sick? I don't know what he sees in that Jackie. You're much better than her, Sue.

**Sue** Well, I'm not very nice to Terry. I tease him all the time. Anyway, Jackie is much prettier than me.

**Kamala** Oh no she's not, Sue. You're just as pretty as she is.

**Sue** Who are you kidding, Kamala? She's taller than me. In fact, she's the tallest girl in our class. She's slimmer than me and she's got nicer hair.

**Kamala** That's not true. She is tall but she's not as pretty as you. She hasn't got friendly eyes or your lovely smile. Anyway, have a look at this article in this magazine.

**Sue** Can I borrow it?…That's it. We'll see who's the best. I'm going shopping.

**At the shops**

**Kamala** Isn't it funny?
The shortest dresses are always the most expensive. Do you like those dresses over there?

**Sue** No, I want something more modern. Mmm, I like this. What do you think, Kam?

**Kamala** But it's £30, Sue. There must be something less expensive here.

**Sue** I want the best. And now I need…

**At the disco**

**Jackie** This is the worst disco in the world, Terry. Let's go somewhere else. It can't be worse than this.

**Terry** (thinks) I haven't got any money…Oh, all right. Just a minute.

**Kamala**  He's coming over, Sue. And Jackie doesn't look very happy.

**Terry**  Hi, Sue. Can you lend me a couple of quid?

**Sue**  Oh…er…Oh yes, of course. Here you are.

**Terry**  Thanks, Sue. You're a real friend. I'll pay you back next week. Oh, I like your dress.

**Sue**  Do you? It's new.

**Terry**  Jackie's got a dress the same as that. She looks great in it. Thanks for the money. See you.

## What do you think?

a  How does Sue feel at the end of the story?

b  What will Sue do now?

## 4  Answer these questions.

a  What does Sue think about Jackie?

b  What does Kamala think about Jackie?

c  What advice does the magazine article give?

d  How much does Sue's new dress cost?

e  What does Jackie think of the disco?

f  Why does Terry borrow money from Sue?

g  What does Terry say about Sue's new dress?

———— optional activity ————

## 5  Close your book. Listen again.

Isn't it funny. The shortest dresses are always the most expensive.

Hi, Sue. Can you lend me a couple of quid?

Oh…er…Oh yes, of course.

Jackie's got a dress the same as that. She looks great in it.

This is the worst disco in the world, Terry. Let's go somewhere else. It can't be worse than this.

I haven't got any money.

## Useful expressions

 **How do you say these expressions in your language?**

**Isn't it funny?**

**Who are you kidding?**

**Doesn't it make you sick?**

**I don't know what he sees in her.**

**I'll pay you back next week.**

**Can you lend me a...?**

**a couple of quid**

 **a** Work in groups of four. Each person takes one of the parts.

**b** Read the dialogue.

─── optional activity ───

### FOLLOW UP

 **Use the words below to complete the conversation.**

fault  than  Terry  what's  less  she's
much  teases  you're  looks  magazine
know  article  sees  more  think

**Casey**  Wow, Sue ................. great this evening. ................. she up to?

**Kam**  She read an ................. in a magazine. She's trying to be ................. attractive than Jackie. It's all because of ................. .

**Casey**  I don't ................. what Terry ................. in Jackie. Sue's ................. better ................. her. She's nicer and ................. more intelligent.

**Kam**  We know that, but Terry doesn't ................. that those things are important. But it isn't all his ................. . I mean, Sue ................. him all the time.

**Casey**  Well I think Terry needs an article in a ................. called 'Can you be ................. stupid?'

**Kam**  Oh Casey, ................. so funny.

## LANGUAGE WORK

# The comparative and superlative ►7.1

 **Look at the picture. Complete the sentences with these words.**

shortest  taller  shorter  tallest

**a** Sue is ................. than Kamala. Jackie is the

................. .

**b** Sue is ................. than Jackie. Kamala is the

................. .

tall**er**, short**er**   We call this the **comparative**.
tall**est**, short**est**   We call this the **superlative**.

**2 a** Complete this table with words from the Victoria Road story.

| adjective | comparative | superlative |
|---|---|---|
| tall | .................... | .................... |
| slim | .................... | slimmest |
| short | shorter | .................... |
| ............ | .................... | nicest |
| pretty | .................... | prettiest |
| good | .................... | .................... |
| bad | .................... | .................... |
| modern | .................... | most modern |
| ............ | more expensive | .................... |
| attractive | .................... | most attractive |

**b** When do we use 'more' and 'most'? Count the number of syllables.

**Exception:** For two-syllable words ending in 'y', change 'y' to 'i' and add 'er' or 'est'.

**c** Work in groups. Add as many words as possible to the table. See which group can add the most in two minutes.

Find nine differences between these two pictures.

Example
*In picture B the shop assistant's hair is shorter.*

— optional activities —

**4** Choose two of your friends or members of your family. Write down ten differences between them.

Examples
John is nicer than Carl.
Carl has got darker hair.

**FOLLOW UP**

**5** Write the answers to Exercise 4.

## Spot the difference

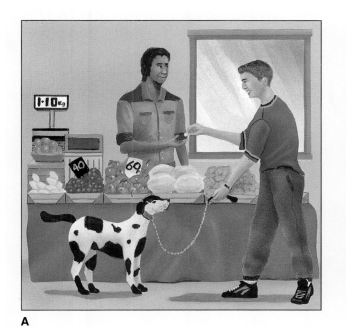

A

B

# READING

**1** Look at the pictures. Match these dates to the correct pictures.

1912   1927   1938
1957   1965   1970
1979   1991

**2** Read the text and check your ideas.

# 20th century fashion

❖ **Before the First World War** fashions did not change very quickly. Men wore dark suits. They had short hair and moustaches were popular. Women wore long dresses with a very narrow waist. They had long hair.

❖ **In the Roaring Twenties** dresses and hair became much shorter. People saw women's knees for the first time! A straight figure with no waist or bust was fashionable. Men wore trousers with very wide legs called Oxford Bags.

❖ **In the 1930s and 40s** hair, dresses, and coats became longer again. Men's fashion didn't change very much. Men wore a suit, a tie, and usually a hat, too. Moustaches went out of fashion.

❖ **In the 1950s** people were richer and teenagers spent a lot of money on clothes. Men wore long jackets in very bright colours – pink, orange, or yellow – and very tight trousers. For women jumpers and blouses with wide skirts and short socks were the fashion. Both men and women wore shoes with long pointed toes. The women's shoes had high stiletto heels.

❖ **The 1960s** were the time of the mini-skirt and long boots. For the first time in the twentieth century men had long hair – the famous Beatle haircut.

❖ **In the late 1960s and the early 70s** the colourful hippy style was in. Women wore loose maxi-skirts or maxi-dresses. Men wore jeans and brightly coloured shirts or T-shirts. Very long hair was fashionable for men and women, and beards became more common (but only for men).

❖ **The late 70s** brought teenagers with punk hairstyles in red, blue, purple, and green, and brightly coloured makeup.

❖ **In the late 1980s and early 90s** loose, casual clothes were in fashion – baggy trousers, a loose sweatshirt, and a baseball cap (usually back to front). Sports clothes like tracksuits and trainers were very fashionable too.

58

**3**

**a** Make a list of all the names of clothes in the text.

**b** Find one example of each item on the pictures.

# Clothes (plurals) ▶7.2

**4** Look:

*I like **this** dress, but **it's** too small.*

*I like **these** jeans, but **they're** too tight.*

**a** What do you notice about **jeans**? Compare the two sentences carefully.

**b** Some names of clothes are always plural. Put these words in the correct column.

| | | | |
|---|---|---|---|
| skirt | tights | bra | vest |
| trousers | jumper | knickers | shorts |
| t-shirt | shirt | underpants | suit |

| singular | always plural (no singular) |
|---|---|
| | |

**5** Look at the pictures.

**a** Choose two of the men and two of the women. Write descriptions of their clothes. Don't show them to your partner.

**b** Read your descriptions to your partner. Can he/she guess the correct pictures?

— optional activities —

**6** What do you think of these fashions? Which do you like or dislike? Why?

**FOLLOW UP**

**7** What do you like wearing:

● every day?
● for parties or going out?

What are you wearing now? Describe your own clothes.

59

# LISTENING

## *A sound journey*

Last Saturday John and Sarah went shopping in town.

 **1 a** 📼 **Listen and say these names.**

| | | |
|---|---|---|
| shoe shop | post office | bus stop |
| department store | chemist's | clothes shop |
| record shop | hairdresser's | |

**b** Look at the pictures. Match the names to the places.

 **2 a** 📼 **Listen and match the conversations to the pictures.**

**b** Which places didn't they visit?

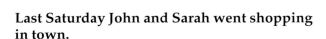 **3 What can you remember?**

**a** What happened in each place that they visited?

**b** What sizes and prices were mentioned?

**c** Listen again and check your ideas.

## A pair of . . . ▶7.2

 **a Look.**

a pair of shorts     three pairs of shorts

**b** Look at the pictures on pages 58–9. How many of each of the following can you find?

trousers   jeans   shoes   skirts   hats   boots

---
#### optional activities
---

 **A game. For my holidays . . .**

**A** 'For my holidays I packed a shirt.'
**B** 'For my holidays I packed a shirt and two pairs of trousers.'
**C** 'For my holidays I packed a shirt, two pairs of trousers and three dresses.'
etc. . . .

### FOLLOW UP

 **Describe the shopping trip. Say:**

● where they went.
● what they wanted.
● what happened.

**Start like this.**
*First they took the bus. They got off at the Square and then they went to . . .*

# INTERACTION

## Shopping

 **1** **Put this dialogue in the correct order.**

**A** Yes. Have you got these trainers in a size 9, please?

**B** They're £54.99.

**C** Thank you very much. £60.00 – that's £5.01 change. Goodbye.

**D** Let me see. Yes, here you are. Do you want to try them on?

**E** That's £54.99, please.

**F** Goodbye.

**G** Here you are.

**H** Yes, please.

**I** Can I help you?

**J** Are they comfortable?

**K** Fine. I'll take them.

**L** Yes, they fit very well. How much are they?

**2** **Role play your dialogue with a partner.**

## Sizes

 **3** **British and Continental sizes are not the same. Look at these tables.**

| waist, chest, bust | | shirts | |
|---|---|---|---|
| **British** | **Continental** | **British** | **Continental** |
| 28 | 71 | 13 | 34 |
| 30 | 76 | 14 | 36 |
| 32 | 81 | 15 | 38 |
| 34 | 86 | 15½ | 39/40 |
| 36 | 91 | 16 | 41 |
| 38 | 97 | 16½ | 42 |
| 40 | 102 | 17 | 43 |
| 42 | 107 | | |

| shoes | | | |
|---|---|---|---|
| **British** | **Continental** | **British** | **Continental** |
| 3 | 36 | 8 | 42 |
| 4 | 37 | 8½ | 42/43 |
| 5 | 38 | 9 | 43 |
| 5½ | 39 | 9½ | 44 |
| 6 | 39/40 | 10 | 44/45 |
| 6½ | 40 | 10½ | 45 |
| 7 | 40/41 | 11 | 46 |
| 7½ | 41 | | |

**a** Write down your measurements in British and Continental sizes.

**b** Ask people in your class.

Example
*What size shoes do you take?*

**4** **Make new shopping dialogues for these items. Use your own sizes.**

£7.95

£62.99

£34.40

£54.99

─── optional activity ───

**FOLLOW UP**

**5** **Write one of your dialogues from Exercise 4.**

# PROJECT

## Oral presentations

**1** In this project you must speak and listen. Here are some rules for a good oral presentation.

- Everything must be ready before the presentations start. Practise your presentation in your group first. Check your pronunciation with your teacher.
- Don't sit in your group. If you do, you won't listen to the other presentations. You'll talk about your own.
- Speak loudly and clearly.
- Be brief. Long presentations are boring.
- Don't talk while other people are presenting.

## *Today's fashions*

**2** Organize a class fashion show.

a Work in groups of four.

b One group are the organizers. They must:

- prepare an introduction to the show
- organize the presentations
- organize the voting
- announce the winners
- thank everyone and close the show

c All the other groups must:

- Choose two models. They can be yourselves or pictures from magazines.
- Prepare your presentation. Describe what each model is wearing.

Example

*Roger is wearing a red plastic jacket with a black collar. The jacket is £52 from 'Fashion Store'. You can also get this jacket in blue and green. With the jacket, Roger's wearing multi-coloured trousers with a black belt and a red and yellow shirt. The trousers and the shirt are both from 'Top Clothes'. The trousers are £28 and the shirt is £16.*

d Each group presents its models and describes their clothes.

e Each group chooses the three best outfits. (You can't choose your own.)

f Each group gives and explains its choices.

g Count the votes and announce the winners.

## Learning *diary* 7

**What have you learnt in this unit?**

A Do the self-check in the Workbook. Check any grammar problems in the reference section on pages 101–107.

B What things have you done in pairs or groups in this unit? What did you like or dislike about these activities? Did you use any of the ideas that you discussed in Learning to learn on page 53? Did they help you?

**Complete your learning diary.**

▶ Pronunciation: page 99

# 8 revision

---

**past continuous**
**future with 'will'**
**first conditionals**
**comparatives**
**clothes**

---

**1** Look at the items above.

**a** Write down two things that you know about each one.

**b** Check your ideas in the Grammar reference.

**2 a** Read this news report.

> Yesterday there was a bank robbery in West London. The police are looking for three people - two men and a woman. Here is a description of them .....

**b** Look at the picture. Write the description of the people that the police are looking for.

**c** Compare the two men and their clothes. Use these words:

short, slim, dark, worried, heavy, casual, colourful

**3** A woman thinks that she saw the robbers at the station.

**a** Complete her conversation with the police. Put the verbs in brackets into the past simple or past continuous tense.

**Policeman** What ........... they ........... , when you

first ........... them? (do/see)

**Woman** They ............ on the train. (get)

**Policeman** ........... anything ........... on the train? (happen)

**Woman** Yes. When I ........... to go to the restaurant

car, they ........... into the suitcase. (get up/look)

**Policeman** ............ you ........... anything? (see)

**Woman** No, when they ............ me, they ........... the

suitcase immediately. (see/close)

**Policeman** Where ........... they ........... ? (get off)

**Woman** At Birmingham Airport.

**b**  Listen and check your ideas.

**4** Complete what the policeman says. Use these verbs:

stop    be    reach    not find    hurry
phone    leave    get

**a** If they ..................... the country, we .....................
them easily.

**b** But we ..................... them, if they .....................
still at the airport.

**c** If we ..................... the airport police, they
..................... all the flights.

**d** We ..................... the airport in ten minutes if we
..................... .

**5** The two men and the woman are at the airport. Say whether they will or won't do these things.

- try to leave the country   ● use false passports
- travel together   ● talk to the police
- change their clothes   at the airport

--- optional activity ---

FOLLOW UP

**6** Write an ending for the story.

63

## interaction
## vocabulary

 **Complete these dialogues.**

**a Passenger** Birmingham, ..........................

**Ticket clerk** ......................... or return?

**Passenger** Return, please.

**Ticket clerk** That .............. be £17, please.

**Passenger:** What ........... is the next ...........?

**Ticket clerk** Half ............ nine.

**Passenger** And ............ time is the train

back?

**Ticket clerk** If you .............. the 9.45 from

Birmingham, .............. get back at 11 o'clock.

**Passenger** Is .............. the last train?

**Ticket clerk** No, there's a train ............

midnight, but you ........... get back till two o'clock

........... the morning.

**Passenger** Thank you.

**b Assistant** Can I .............. you?

**Customer** Yes. I'd like a ............ of jeans,

please.

**Assistant** Sure. What ....... do you ............?

**Customer** 32.

**Assistant** Here ....... are. Do you ............ to

try ................ on?

**Customer** Yes, please.

**Assistant** Are ............ all right?

**Customer** No, .............. too big. ..............

you got them in a smaller ..............?

**Assistant** Yes. Try ........ .

**Customer** Oh, yes. These are ............ . I'll

take them. How ......... are they?

**Assistant** .............. £43.60.

**Customer** Here you ..............

**Assistant** Thank ............ . That's £1.40

........... .

**2 Find the odd one out in each list. Explain your choice.**

**a** hat   jeans   T-shirt   socks   dress

**b** waist   moustache   knees   makeup   bust

**c** Asia   India   Europe   Africa   America

**d** summer   winter   equator   autumn   spring

**e** airport   luggage   station   shop   bus stop

**f** prettiest   tallest   better   worst   shortest

**g** bus   train   motorbike   taxi   ticket

**h** most   south   east   north   west

**i** pink   purple   orange   yellow   narrow

--- optional activity ---

**4 Look at the song.**

**a** What do you think the missing words are?

**b** What do you think the title is?

**c** 📼 Listen and check your ideas.

**d** Listen again. Complete the song.

### G.... a.... o....

You s............. that you love me
All of the t............ .
You say that you n............ me,
You'll a............ be mine.

Chorus

A............ I'm feeling glad all over.
Yes, I............ glad all over.
B............ , I'm glad all over,
So glad you're m............ .

I'll make you h............ .
You'll n............ be blue.
Y............ have no sorrow.
I'll always b............ true.

Other girls may t............ to take me a............ ,
But you k............ here by your s............ I will stay.
I, I w............ stay.

O............ love will last now
Till the e............ of time,
B............ this love now
Is o............ yours and mine.

▶ **Pronunciation: page 99**

# Main grammar point:
## The present perfect tense

**Terry**  Have you seen Jackie today?

**Sue**  No. I saw her yesterday, but I haven't seen her today.

**Vince**  Her Mum's taken her to the airport and she hasn't come back yet.

## Learning objectives

**Learning to learn:** Dealing with problems

**Victoria Road:** Talking about past events that affect the present

**Language work:** The present perfect tense ▶ 9.1–3

**Reading:** Reading for specific information
Finding out about London
Talking about what you have done

**Listening:** Listening and predicting events
Comparing the present perfect and the past
simple tenses ▶ 9.4

**Interaction:** Talking about experiences

**Guided writing:** Reference

## Ω Learning to learn: *Dealing with problems*

**a**  What problems do you have with learning English? What things do you find difficult?

**b**  In the class, or in a group, choose a common problem. Write some advice for dealing with it.

Example
*People speak too fast and I can't understand all the words.*

- Don't try to understand every word. Try to understand the general meaning first.
- Listen to things more than once if possible.
- Ask people to repeat or speak more slowly.
- Don't be afraid to say 'I don't understand'.

# Jackie's cousin arrives

**1** Look at this episode. Who is the new character? Where is he from? What is wrong with Terry?

**2** Connect the subjects to the endings.

| | |
|---|---|
| Greg | is looking for Jackie. |
| Mr Moore | saw her yesterday. |
| Terry | has gone to the airport. |
| Sue | is arriving today. |
| Jackie | thinks that Jackie's cousin is a girl. |
| Terry | is pleased to meet Terry. |
| Terry | brought Terry a cowboy hat from the USA. |
| Jackie's cousin | throws the hat in the bin. |

Her cousin from America is arriving today.

I didn't know she had an American cousin.

Have you seen Jackie this morning?

No. I saw her in town yesterday, but I haven't seen her today.

My dad's been to America, you know. He was there last summer.

I know. I've seen the cowboy hat on your bedroom wall.

**3** 🔊 Listen and follow in your book.

**Terry** Have you seen Jackie this morning?

**Sue** No. I saw her in town yesterday, but I haven't seen her today.

**Vince** She's gone to the airport.

**Terry** What has she gone there for?

**Vince** Her cousin from America is arriving today.

**Terry** I didn't know she had an American cousin. When did she go?

**Vince** She went with her mum at about 8 o'clock. I met them when I was doing my paper round.

### Later

**Terry** Hi, Jackie. Has your cousin arrived?

**Jackie** Yes, but the plane was late. So we've only just got back.

**Terry** My dad's been to America, you know. He was there last summer.

**Jackie** I know. I've seen the cowboy hat on your bedroom wall.

**Terry** Oh yes. You must introduce me. I've never met anyone from America. What's her name?

**Jackie** *His* name is Greg. He's brought me lots of things from the States. You'll like him, Terry. Oh, here he is now.

**Jackie** Greg, this is Terry.

**Greg** Hi, Terry. Pleased to meet you. I've heard all about you from Jackie.

**Terry** Hello. Good Lord. Is that the time? I must go. See you around.

### Later

**Vince** Terry. What have you done with your cowboy hat?

Speech bubbles in image 1:
"I've never met anyone from America. What's her name?"
"*His* name is Greg."

Speech bubbles in image 4:
"Greg, this is Terry."
"Hi, Terry. Pleased to meet you."

Speech bubble in image 5:
"Terry. What have you done with your cowboy hat?"

## What do you think?

a How does Terry feel about Greg?

b Why has he thrown the hat in the bin?

**4 Answer these questions.**

a When did Sue see Jackie?

b Where has she gone?

c When did she go?

d How does Vince know?

e When did Terry's dad go to America?

f What is Terry surprised about?

g What has Terry done with his hat?

── optional activity ──

 Close your book. Listen again.

## Useful expressions

**6** How do you say these expressions in your language?

**you know**

**Here he is.**

**See you around.**

**Is that the time?**

**Pleased to meet you.**

**You must introduce me.**

**We've only just got back.**

**7** a Work in groups of three. One person is Terry, one is Sue and Jackie, and one is Greg and Vince.

b Read the dialogue.

── optional activity ──

**FOLLOW UP**

 Write the answers to Exercise 4 in full.

# LANGUAGE WORK

## The present perfect tense ▶9.1–3

 **Look at these sentences.**

**Have** you **seen** Jackie this morning?
I **haven't seen** her today.
She**'s gone** to the airport.

We call this the **present perfect** tense.

**Find more examples in the Victoria Road story.**

> The present perfect shows an activity in the past which tells us something about the present.

Examples
*I haven't seen her today.*
= I don't know where she is now.
*She has gone to the airport.*
= She is at the airport now.
*He has thrown his hat in the bin.*
= The hat is in the bin now.

 **How do we make the present perfect?**

**The present perfect has two parts.**

| He | has | arrived |
|----|-----|---------|
| | the verb 'to have' | a past participle |

**a** Complete this table with the correct parts of the verb 'to have'.

| I | have | arrived. |
|---|------|----------|
| You | 've | recorded many hits. |
| We | ..... .... | painted the hall. |
| They | haven't | collected some souvenirs. |
| | | practised on the computer. |
| He | ......... | received a letter. |
| She | ......... | worked here for ten years. |
| It | has not ......... | appeared on TV. |

**b** All the verbs in the table have regular past participles. How do we make the regular past participle?

**c** A lot of verbs have irregular past participles.

Example
*I haven't **seen** Jackie today.*

Find the past participles of these verbs in the story.

| meet | bring |
|------|-------|
| hear | do |
| have | throw |
| get | |

**d** Complete the rule with two of these.

the verb 'to be'
the verb 'to have'
the past tense
the infinitive
the past participle

> To make the present perfect we use ...............
> ................................... **plus** .....................
> ................................... .

 **Complete these sentences. Put the verbs in brackets into the present perfect tense.**

Example
*Vince has seen Jackie today. (see)*

**a** Terry and Sue ................. her. (not see)

**b** She ................. to the airport. (go)

**c** They ................. back yet. (not get)

**d** Jackie's American cousin ................. for a holiday. (come)

**e** The people in Victoria Road ................. her cousin before. (not meet)

**f** Jackie ................. Terry about her cousin. (not tell)

**g** Terry ................. to the States. (not be)

**h** Terry's father ................. there. (be)

## The present perfect tense: questions ▶9.2

**5** **a** Complete these sentences from the story.

................. you ................. Jackie this
morning? (see)

.................your cousin ............... ? (arrive)

**b** Make a statement and a question with each group of words.

**A** you/to/have/the/States/been
**B** the/gone/airport/has/she/to

**c** Complete this rule.

> To make questions in the present perfect we
> put ........... or ........... in front of the ........... .

**6** Work in pairs. Look at the list in Exercise 4. Ask Greg questions.

Examples
**A** *'Have you visited the Tower of London?'*
**B** *'No, I haven't.'*
**A** *'Have you telephoned your parents?'*
**B** *'Yes, I have.'*

**7** Use the cues. Ask your partner about what he/she has done this week.

Example
*Have you seen a film?*
*Yes, I have./No, I haven't.*

see a film                    help with the housework
play a sport                  have an interesting dream
be ill                        watch any good
buy anything                    programmes on TV
do all your homework

**4** Greg has been in England for three days. Here are the things he wants to do while he is in England. Look at the list and say what Greg has and hasn't done.

Examples
He hasn't visited the Tower of London.
He has telephoned his parents.

- ☐ visit the Tower of London
- ☑ telephone his parents
- ☐ send postcards to his friends
- ☑ have a rest
- ☐ get presents for his family
- ☐ travel on the London Underground
- ☐ spend a day at Covent Garden
- ☑ meet Jackie's friends
- ☑ watch a cricket match
- ☑ change some money
- ☑ take a lot of photographs
- ☑ unpack his suitcase
- ☐ see Buckingham Palace
- ☐ buy some/any new clothes

─── optional activity ───

**FOLLOW UP**

**8** What have you done this week? Write ten things.

## READING

# A visit to London

 **Greg and Jackie have been to London for the day. They have done these things.**

- They have seen the Queen's crown.
- They have had lunch with a brontosaurus.
- Greg has taken photographs of Jackie with the Prime Minister and Paul McCartney.
- They have looked at photographs of the stars.

**Look at this list of things to do in London. Which places have Greg and Jackie visited? How do you know?**

**Remember:** You don't have to understand every word.

 **Match the pictures to the places.**

 **Find the answers to these questions.**

a  What is the Palace of Westminster?

b  What is the Prime Minister's address?

c  Where is the Natural History Museum?

d  Where can you stand with one foot in the western hemisphere and one foot in the eastern hemisphere?

e  At how many places can you:
  - buy something to eat?
  - buy souvenirs?

### W O R D   W O R K

**4 Find all the names of places in the texts.**

Examples
*museum    palace    zoo*

## Things to see in London

A

### ▶ Downing Street

Number 10 Downing Street has been the home of the British Prime Minister since 1735.

### ▶ The Houses of Parliament

Its official name is the Palace of Westminster. Most of the building was built in 1840 after a fire in 1834 destroyed the old palace. At the north end of the building by Westminster Bridge is the famous clock tower, Big Ben. In fact Big Ben is really the name of the bell in the tower not the clock.

### ▶ The Tower of London

London's oldest building. Since it was built by William the Conqueror in the 11th century, this castle has been a royal palace, a prison, a place of execution, a zoo, the Royal Mint and an observatory. Today it's a museum and houses the Crown Jewels. Gift shop.

*Open Monday–Saturday 9.30–5.45*
*Sundays 2–5.45*

### ▶ The Natural History Museum

Situated in Kensington. One of London's greatest museums. A huge collection of animals and plants, including a quarter of a million butterflies, a blue whale and the famous dinosaur skeletons. Cafeteria, gift shop and book shop.

*Open daily 10–5.45*

### ▶ Madame Tussauds, Marylebone Road

This famous waxworks has models of famous people from pop stars to prime ministers. Displays of battles and Chamber of Horrors. Gift shop.

*Open every day 10–5.30, except Christmas Day*

### ▶ The Royal Observatory, Greenwich

10 miles outside London on a hill above the River Thames. The Observatory contains telescopes and displays about astronomy, including Halley's Comet and Black Holes. The international meridian line runs through the Observatory. Video theatre and souvenir shop. Picnic in Greenwich Park. Take a river boat to Greenwich from Westminster Bridge.

*Open 10.30 am to 5.30 pm*
*Closed 25–28 December*

**B**

**C**

**D**

**E**

**F**

— optional activities —

 **5** **Work in pairs. Make your own day out. You can visit two places.**

**a** Write down two things that you have done or seen on your day out.

> Example
> *We have seen Big Ben.*

**b** Give your things to another pair. They must say where you have been.

> Example
> *You have been to the Houses of Parliament.*

**FOLLOW UP**

 **6** **Answer these questions.**

**a** Where can you see butterflies?

**b** Which building is nine hundred years old?

**c** Which place opens at half past ten in the morning?

**d** Find two places where you can see the Prime Minister.

**e** Which place is not open on Sunday mornings?

## LISTENING

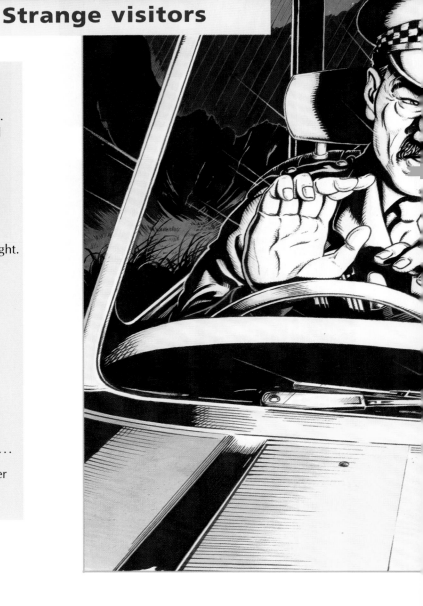

**Strange visitors**

**1** Read this.

One night in September 1983 Constable David (Scottie) McLintock and Constable Peter Owen were on patrol in the mountains of North Wales. Some thieves were stealing sheep from the local farms. The two policemen were looking for the thieves.

**DJ** It's 3.30 am on Thursday 23 September and you're listening to the *Late Late Show* on Radio Wales ...

**Owen** We've been on patrol for six hours tonight. We haven't seen anything.

**McLintock** We were on patrol for six hours yesterday. We didn't see anything then. Call Sergeant Jones.

**Owen** OK. Car CX7 to base. Car CX7 to base. We've had no luck, Sarge. The thieves haven't come.

**Sergeant** All right. Come back to the station.

**Owen** Mmm. We're on our way back to a nice cup of tea at the station now. I don't know why ...

**McLintock** Wait a minute, Taff. What's that over there? I've just seen a light by the old mine.

# The present perfect and past simple ▶9.5

 **a** Look at these sentences.
What tense is used in the first two sentences?
What tense is used in the second two sentences?

> We**'ve been** on patrol for six hours **tonight**. We **haven't seen** anything.
> We **were** on patrol for six hours **yesterday**. We **didn't see** anything **then**.

**b** Why are they different? What times are they about?

**c** Copy and complete this diagram with the names of the tenses.

present
present perfect
past

............ Present
............

**d** Look at what has happened to the policemen tonight. What happened yesterday?

Example
We've been on patrol for six hours tonight.
*We were on patrol for six hours yesterday.*

We've been on patrol for six hours tonight.
We haven't seen anything.
The thieves haven't come.
We've had no luck.
We've searched the hills.
We've talked to all the farmers.
The weather has been very cold.
We've listened to the radio.

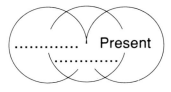 **a** What was the light by the old mine?
What do you think happened?

**b**  Listen and check your ideas.

## 4 Put these in the correct order.

return to the station
car engine stops
look for thieves
see light behind them
see a light
look at the calendar
light disappears
call base
light gets closer
start the car

## 5 What do you think?

a What has happened to the two men?

b What has happened at home while the two men have been away?

─── optional activity ───

### FOLLOW UP

## 6 Use the cues from Exercise 4. Tell the story of McLintock and Owen. Begin like this.

*Constables McLintock and Owen were on patrol. They were looking for thieves...*

# INTERACTION

## Experiences

### 1 a Look at this dialogue. What tense is used:

● in the first question and answer?
● in the rest of the dialogue.

**b Why are the different tenses used?**

**Jane** Have you ever met anyone famous?
**David** Yes, I have.
**Jane** Who did you meet?
**David** Steven Spielberg.
**Jane** How did you meet him?
**David** He was making a movie where we were on holiday.
**Jane** What did you do?
**David** I asked him for his autograph.

### 2 Ask your partner about his/her experiences.

**a** Look at these cues. What questions will you ask first?

meet anyone famous
speak English outside the classroom
see a film in English
visit another country
lose anything important
have an accident
fly in an aeroplane
be embarrassed
win anything
do anything dangerous

**b** If your partner answers 'yes', what other questions can you ask?

### 3 Work with a partner.

**A:** Ask the questions. Find out as much as possible about each experience.
**B:** Answer A's questions. (You needn't be honest.)

### 4 Tell the class what you have found out about your partner's life.

─── optional activity ───

### FOLLOW UP

### 5 Look at the list in Exercise 2. Write about your experiences. Give some details about the things that you have done.

Examples
*I've never met anyone famous.*
*I've spoken English outside the classroom. Last summer some tourists asked me the way.*

73

# GUIDED WRITING

## Reference

**1** When we write a text we link some of the sentences together. In unit 6 you looked at linkers like 'when', 'and' and 'but'. We can also use reference to link sentences.

**a** Look at the underlined words in the first paragraph of the boy's essay about his life. What do they refer to?

Example
*'It' refers to 'Hadley'.*

**b** What kind of words are used for reference in the essay?

**c** Find more examples in the other paragraphs. What do they refer to?

## *My life*

**2** Write an essay about your life.

**a** Look at the boy's essay. What is the topic of each paragraph?

**b** What other topics could you write about?

**c** What tenses does he use? What does he use each one for?

**d** Write about your life. Organize your essay into paragraphs and try to use linkers and reference.

▶ **Pronunciation: page 99**

### My life • • • • • • • • • • • • • • • • • • • • •

I haven't lived in the same house all my life. I was born in a town called Hadley. It's in the north of England. But when I was four, my dad got a job in London and we moved down here. At first we had a house in Holland Road, but then my baby sister was born and we needed a bedroom for her. So we moved to a bigger house in Barton Street. We've lived here for three years now. I like our house. It's quite old and it's got a big garden.

I've seen some changes in our neighbourhood. When I can first remember, there was a small factory at the end of Barton Street. Two years ago it closed down. There are some new houses there now. I'm glad that they built the houses, because my best friend, Tony, moved into one of them. Before that he lived a few miles away, so I only saw him at school.

We usually take our holidays in Britain. I've only been abroad once. I went skiing with the school trip. It was great. I learned to ski quite quickly and I really enjoyed it.

My hobby is rowing. I've done it for about five years now. I've won two competitions. I won one of them last year and one the year before.

**Learning *diary*** 9

What have you learnt in this unit?

**A** Do the self-check in the Workbook. Check any grammar problems in the reference section on pages 101–107.

**B** What problems did you have in this unit? Did you use any of the advice from the Learning to learn section on page 65?

**Complete your learning diary.**

# Main grammar point:
## Talking about quantity

*Have you got any money?*

*Why?*

*I want to make some pizzas for the party and we haven't got any cheese.*

*How many pizzas are you making?*

*Just a few.*

*How much cheese do you need?*

*Just a bit.*

*food*

**10**

## Learning objectives

| | |
|---|---|
| **Learning to learn:** | Planning your revision |
| **Victoria Road:** | Talking about food |
| **Language work:** | some/any ► 10.1<br>Countable and uncountable nouns ► 10.2<br>a bit/a few/a lot of |
| **Reading:** | Reading and understanding a menu<br>Food vocabulary |
| **Listening:** | Understanding a recipe<br>Talking about quantities and containers |
| **Interaction:** | Ordering a meal |
| **Guided writing:** | Sequence linkers |

## ☺ Learning to learn: *Planning your revision*

**a**  Look through the book and your Learning Diary. Decide these things:

  ● what do you need to concentrate on?
  ● how much time do you have available?
  ● how much time should you give to each thing?

**b**  Make a timetable and make sure you stick to it.

# Jackie's surprise

**1** ▼ **What do you remember? What happened in the last part of the story? Look back at page 66 and check your ideas.**

**2** ▼ **a** Match these things to the correct pictures.

> big mouths    Fat Cat    hamburgers
> the States    money    September

**b** What do the people say about each of the things.

*Come on, you lot. We're going to the Fat Cat. Are you coming? We'll pay.*

*I'm bored and I'm broke. Have you got any money, Sue?*

*I've already lent you some money this month, Terry.*

**1**

**2**

**3** 🔊 **Listen and follow in your book.**

**Casey** What shall we do?

**Terry** I'm bored and I'm broke. Have you got any money, Sue?

**Sue** I've already lent you some money this month, Terry. And I bought some birthday presents yesterday. So I haven't got any money now.

**Terry** How much money have you got, Case?

**Casey** I've got a bit, but I've got to buy a lot of things for my bike. I wish Jackie was here. She's always got a lot of money.

**Sue** Here she is now with Greg.

**Terry** Oh no, not Buffalo Bill. Is he still here?

**Jackie** Come on, you lot. We're going to the Fat Cat. Are you coming? We'll pay.

### In the cafe

**Waitress** Can I help you?

**Greg** Yes please. Could we have two glasses of Coke, two cups of tea, and I'll have a glass of milk.

**Waitress** I'm sorry. How many cups of tea did you want?

**Sue** Two.

**Waitress** Do you want anything to eat?

**Greg** Yes, can we have two sandwiches – one ham, one chicken – one cheeseburger with a plate of french fries – I mean chips. And two hamburgers.

**Terry** Have you got any packets of crisps?

**Waitress** No, I'm sorry, we haven't.

**Terry** That's okay. Thanks.

### Later

**Greg** You can't get real cheeseburgers in England, you know. Now, in an American hamburger we only use the best steak and it doesn't have just a few onions, a bit of salad and one slice of cheese. It has at least two slices of cheese, a lot of onions and a lot of salad, too – tomatoes, lettuce, cucumber and…

**Sue** Mmm. It must be very big.

**Terry** Well, Americans have got big mouths, haven't they?

**Jackie** Don't be childish, Terry.

**Greg** Anyway, Jackie. You'll see for yourself in September.

**Terry** Why? What's happening in September?

**Jackie**  Oh, haven't you heard? I'm going to live in the States for a year with Greg's family. Isn't it wonderful?

**What do you think?**

a  What does Terry think about Greg? How do you know?

b  How does each of them feel at the end?

▼ **Answer these questions.**

a  Why hasn't Sue got any money?

b  What must Casey do?

c  Who is with Jackie?

d  What does Terry call Greg? Why?

e  What does Jackie offer to do?

f  What do they order to drink?

g  Why doesn't Greg like British cheeseburgers?

h  How will Jackie find out about American hamburgers?

―――――― optional activity ――――――

▼ **Close your book. Listen again.**

# Useful expressions

**6** How do you say these expressions in your language?

> I'm broke.
>
> Come on, you lot.
>
> Could we have…?
>
> Haven't you heard?
>
> You'll see for yourself.
>
> I wish Jackie was here.
>
> I've got to … (= I must)

**7**

a Work in groups of four. One person is Terry, one is Greg, one is Sue and Jackie, and one is the waitress and Casey.

b Read the dialogue.

--- optional activities ---

## FOLLOW UP

**8**  Write the answers to the questions in Exercise 4 in full.

**9**  Some words are different in British and American English.

a Here are some examples.

b Use a dictionary. Find the American words for these.

| | |
|---|---|
| flat | film |
| cinema | colour |
| lift | motorway |
| shop | programme |

# LANGUAGE WORK

## some/any  ►10.1

**1**

a Complete these sentences with 'some' or 'any'.

Have you got ……….. money?

I haven't got ……….. money.

I bought ……….. birthday presents yesterday.

b When do you use 'some' and when do you use 'any'? Complete this general rule.

> We use ……………… in questions and negative statements.
>
> We use ……………… in positive statements.

**2**  Use 'some' or 'any' to complete these sentences.

a I need ……….. new shoes, but I haven't got ……….. money.

b Have you got ……….. brothers or sisters?

c Is there ……….. food in the fridge?

d We didn't get ……….. Maths homework yesterday, but we got ……….. Geography homework.

e There isn't ……….. one at home.

f I haven't got ……….. thing to do.

g I've got ……….. thing in my eye.

h Are there ……….. shops in your street?

i I didn't see ……….. one at the club.

j ……….. one has stolen my purse.

American
french fries
gas
chips
pants
drug store
truck

British
chips
petrol
crisps
trousers
chemist
lorry

# Countable/uncountable nouns ►10.2

**a** **Read this.**

Some nouns are countable. They have a singular and a plural.

| | |
|---|---|
| a person | some people |
| a sandwich | some sandwiches |
| a cup | some cups |

Some nouns are uncountable. They have no plural.

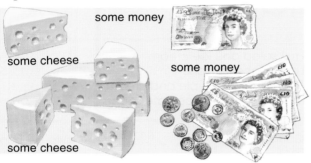

some money

some cheese

some money

some cheese

**b** **Some things are usually uncountable. Look at the lists in Grammar reference 10.2.**

**c** **Are these things countable or uncountable?**

tomatoes

shampoo

stamps

orange juice

bread

pencils

water

wood

apples

meat

soap powder

**d** **Can you think of any more examples for the lists in Grammar reference 10.2?**

**a** **Look at the Victoria Road story again. Find the phrases with these expressions in them.**

**A** a bit of
**B** a few
**C** a lot of
**D** How much . . . ?
**E** How many . . . ?

**b** **Which expressions do we use with countable nouns and which with uncountable nouns?**

--- optional activities ---

**5** **Work in pairs. Use the words in Exercise 3a and c to make dialogues like this:**

> **A** I need some money.
> **B** How much do you need?
> **A** Just a bit. (or Just a little.)

> **A** I need some stamps.
> **B** How many do you need?
> **A** Just a few.

## FOLLOW UP

**6** **When you get home, look in your fridge or cupboard. Which of these are in it? How much is there?/How many are there?**

Examples
*There aren't any onions in our fridge.*
*There is a lot of milk.*
*There are a lot of apples in our cupboard.*
*There isn't any orange juice in our cupboard.*

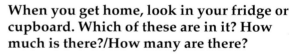

| | |
|---|---|
| onions | tea |
| milk | carrots |
| apples | bananas |
| orange juice | eggs |
| ham | cola |
| cheese | potatoes |
| sausages | tomatoes |
| water | fish |
| coffee | fruit |

# READING

**1** **Look quickly at this menu and find the answers to these questions.**

**a** What is the name of the restaurant?

**b** What kind of food does it sell?

**c** Which of these can't you buy at this restaurant?

soup   tea   bread   chips   mineral water

hamburgers   chocolate cake   ice cream

fruit juice   sandwiches   pancakes

**d** Kamala doesn't eat meat. Which pizzas can she eat?

# Pizza Palace

### STARTERS
| | |
|---|---|
| Home–made tomato soup | 90p |
| Garlic bread | £1.00 |
| Jacket potato with butter | 95p |

#### Salad
Make your own salad from our salad bar: cucumber, tomatoes, onions, lettuce, peppers, sweetcorn, beans — £1.75

### PIZZAS

#### The big one
A traditional pizza with ham, salami sausage, black olives, green peppers and sliced mushrooms — £4.60

#### The taste of the sea
If you like fish, you'll love this pizza. It has tuna, mussels, anchovies and sardines on a traditional cheese and tomato base — £4.40

#### Some like it hot
You get a free glass of water with our special hot pizza: beef, hot chillies, red and green peppers, onions and tomatoes — £4.30

#### Vegetarian delight
A healthy alternative with green peppers, mushrooms and onions on a cheese and tomato pizza — £4.10

#### Hawaiian style
An exotic pizza from the South Seas: ham, chicken, pineapple and sweetcorn — £4.05

#### Traditional
Cheese and tomato — £3.40

**All our pizzas are available with traditional or wholemeal base.**

Why not add some delicious extra toppings to your pizza? Or make a pizza to your own recipe.

#### Extras
Cheese, mushrooms, black olives, green peppers, sweetcorn, pineapple, chicken, onions, salami, tuna, mussels — 30p each

### DESSERTS
| | |
|---|---|
| Fruit salad and ice cream | £2.15 |
| Lemon cheesecake | £1.75 |
| Traditional apple pie and cream | £1.65 |
| Ice cream with chocolate sauce | 95p |

### BEVERAGES
| | |
|---|---|
| Coffee | 64p per cup |
| Tea | 59p per pot |
| Hot chocolate | 55p per cup |

### ICE COLD DRINKS
| | Large | Standard |
|---|---|---|
| Cola | 95p | 80p |
| Diet cola | 95p | 80p |
| Lemonade | 95p | 80p |
| Mineral water | 85p per bottle | |
| Apple juice | 90p | |
| Orange juice | 80p | |

### ALCOHOLIC DRINKS
| | |
|---|---|
| Beer | £1.60 per bottle |
| Red wine | £1.30 per glass |
| White wine | £1.30 per glass |

#### Important note
*We can only serve alcoholic drinks with meals.*
*We cannot serve alcoholic drinks to customers under 18 years of age.*
*Families: See our special Children's Menu.*
*There is no service charge included in your bill.*
*During busy periods we serve only meals.*
*All prices include VAT.*
*Take-away service:*
*All our pizzas are available to take away at a 10% discount on menu prices.*

**2** **Which of the following is not in any of the pizzas?**

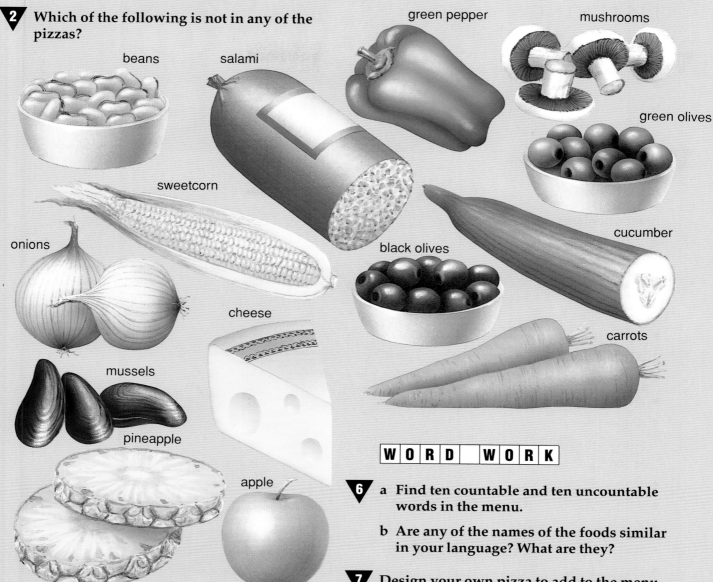

green pepper

mushrooms

beans

salami

green olives

sweetcorn

onions

black olives

cucumber

cheese

carrots

mussels

pineapple

apple

---

**W O R D   W O R K**

**6** a **Find ten countable and ten uncountable words in the menu.**

b **Are any of the names of the foods similar in your language? What are they?**

**7** **Design your own pizza to add to the menu. Give it a name and say what it contains.**

*optional activity*

**3** **Look at this order. Make a list of all the ingredients the chef will need.**

| | |
|---|---|
| 1 × jacket potato | 1 × Taste of the Sea |
| 1 × garlic bread | 1 × Hawaiian style |

**4** **Write down the orders. What will each person pay?**

a Two customers, aged 14, had a starter, a pizza, a dessert, a cold drink and a hot drink each. One had the cheapest possible meal, the other had the most expensive meal possible.

b One customer, aged 20, had a pizza with extra mushrooms and black olives. He had the second most expensive dessert. He didn't buy a drink, because he got a free one.

**5** **Choose your own meal. How much will it cost?**

*optional activity*

**FOLLOW UP**

**8** a **Look through the list of pizzas. Find any words that you do not know. Use a dictionary to find out what they mean.**

b **You are with a friend in England. Your friend does not speak English. Translate the list of pizzas for him/her.**

A: What is worse than finding a worm in your apple?
B: Finding half a worm in your apple.

**1** **Look at the ingredients.**

  **a** What is the recipe for?

  **b** How many do you think it will make?

**2** 📼 **Listen to the recipe. Complete the list of ingredients.**

**Boston burgers**

Serves ........... people

**Ingredients:**

- 750 g minced beef
- 1 ..................
- 1 clove garlic
- 50 g breadcrumbs
- ........... nuts
- 2 ..................
- a little .................. ,
  .................. and
  lemon ..................
- 1 ..................
- 2 ..................
- 4 .................. cheese
- 1 tin ............... rings
- ........... buns

**3** **Look at the pictures.**

  **a** What is happening in each picture?

  **b** Put them in the correct order.

**4** 📼 **Listen to the whole recipe. Check your order.**

— optional activity —

**5** **What do you think about the Boston burger?**

  **a** Is it good for you?

  **b** Should people eat so much when other people are dying of starvation?

# Boston burgers

## A bottle of . . ., etc.

**6 Look.**

a glass of milk     two glasses of milk

**a** These are containers. Match the names to the pictures.

bottle   packet   glass   cup   tin   carton
tube   box

**b** Look at all the pictures in this unit. What can you see in containers?

Examples
*two glasses of cola*
*a tin of pineapple*

**FOLLOW UP**

 Using the pictures, write the recipe for Boston burgers.

---

## INTERACTION

## In a cafe

**1 Look at this dialogue. Put it in the correct order.**

**A** Do you want anything to drink?

**B** Yes, please?

**C** Could I have chicken and chips, please?

**D** One tomato salad. Is that it?

**E** Thank you.

**F** No, thanks. Oh, er, yes. I'll have a tomato salad.

**G** Yes.

**H** Chicken and chips and a glass of milk. Anything else?

**I** I'll have a glass of milk, please.

**2 Look at the menu on page 80.**

Here is the waitress' notebook. Make the dialogues for the orders.

| Pizza Palace | |
|---|---|
| *Order* | |
| Table 10 | 2 x the big one |
| | 1 x fruit salad and ice cream |
| | 2 x pot tea |
| Table 5 | 1 x traditional pizza |
| | 1 x standard lemonade |
| | 1 x soup |

**3 You are in the Pizza Palace. Order something from the menu.**

**FOLLOW UP**

 Write a dialogue for your order at the Pizza Palace.

# GUIDED WRITING

## Sequence linkers

**1** When we write a text with different stages, we use sequence linkers to join some of the stages. Sequence linkers can be one word or a whole phrase.

**a** Look at the recipe for Boston burgers. Complete it with these sequence linkers.

finally     After half an hour     Now     First
When the burgers are cooked     Then
While the burgers are cooking     Then

**b**  Listen to the recipe and check your ideas.

## *Boston Burgers*

**(a)** ........................... , peel and chop the onion, the garlic and the nuts. Put the meat, onion, garlic, breadcrumbs, nuts and eggs in a bowl. Add a little salt, pepper and lemon juice.

**(b)** ........................... mix all the ingredients together with a fork.

With the mixture make four hamburgers. Put the burgers into the refrigerator for 30 minutes. **(c)** ........................... take the cold hamburgers out of the refrigerator and grill (or fry) them for 10 to 15 minutes each side.

**(d)** ........................... , cut the buns in half and toast them. Wash the lettuce and tomatoes. Slice the tomatoes and open the tin of pineapple.

**(e)** ........................... put a bit of lettuce and a few slices of tomato on a bun. Put one burger on top of this. On top of the burger put some more salad. **(f)** ........................... put on a slice of cheese, a pineapple ring and

**(g)** ........................... the top of the bun.

**(h)** ........................... with two hands, pick up the burger and eat.

▶ **Pronunciation: page 99**

## *My favourite recipe*

**2** **Write a recipe for your own favourite kind of food.**

**a** Follow this pattern and use sequence linkers where possible.

Introduce the recipe.
Say why you like it.
Give the ingredients.
Give the instructions.

**b** Show your recipe to other students.

**Note:** When we give ingredients:
We say: fifty grams of breadcrumbs
We write: 50g breadcrumbs

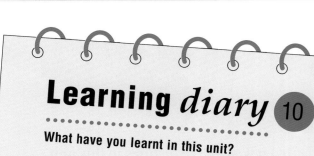

### Learning *diary* 10

What have you learnt in this unit?

**A** Do the self-check in the Workbook. Check any grammar problems in the reference section on pages 101–107.

**B** Look at the revision plan. What must you add from this unit? How well are you keeping to your timetable?

Complete your learning diary.

# Main grammar point:
## The passive

**Active voice**

*Every week record companies **produce** thousands of new records.*

**Passive voice**

*Every week thousands of new records **are produced** by record companies.*

## ℧ Learning to learn: *Ways of revising*

You've made your revision plan. Now how do you revise?

**a** How do you normally revise?

> Examples
> *Test yourself on vocabulary*
> *Write some examples*

**b** Discuss your ideas with other members of the class.
What ways do people find most useful?

# Terry in trouble

**1** **What do you remember? What happened in the last part of the story? Look back at page 76 and check your ideas.**

**2** **a Put these sentences in the correct order to match the picture story.**

1 Sue helps Terry with his homework.

2 Terry is grounded, so he can't go to a party.

3 The school sends a letter to Terry's parents.

4 Terry thinks about Sue and Jackie.

5 Sue comes to see Terry.

6 Terry's teacher is angry with him.

**b Look at each sentence and say why it happens.**

**3** 📼 **Listen and follow in your book.**

**Teacher** Wrong, wrong, wrong. Terry, this is terrible. Macbeth wasn't written by Queen Elizabeth. It was written by Shakespeare. Australia wasn't discovered by Columbus. And look at this in your Geography test. Question: 'Where is coffee found?' Answer: 'In supermarkets.' It's no laughing matter, Terry.

**Terry** Yes, Miss.

**Teacher** Now you were warned last week, Terry. This time a letter will be sent to your parents.

**Later**

**Terry** But, Dad. I've been invited to a party.

**Mr Moore** And I said 'No'. You're grounded, and there'll be no TV until that homework is done properly. And that's that. And your pocket money will be stopped if I get any more letters from school like this. Is that clear? I've had enough of your laziness, young man!

**Later**

**Terry** Oh, hi, Sue. Weren't you invited to the party?

**Sue** Yes, but I didn't want to go, if you...er..., I mean...I was told you couldn't go.

Terry  Did you see Jackie?

Sue  Yes, she was telling everyone about her trip to America.

Terry  Yes, she goes next week.

Sue  Look. Would you like a hand with your Computer Studies homework?

Terry  Yes, please. I'm stuck.

Sue  Look this is very simple. You see, the information is sent by the small computers. It is received by the main computer. It is checked and processed by the main computer. Then the results are stored on the hard disk.

### Later

Terry  Goodnight Sue, and thanks a lot.

Mr Moore  Susan's a nice girl, you know, Terry.

## What do you think?

a  What is wrong with Terry?

b  What does he feel about Jackie?

c  What does he feel about Sue?

d  What will happen now?

**4** **Right, Wrong or Don't know?**

|  | ✓ | ✗ | ? |
|---|---|---|---|
| a  Terry has done well at school. | ❏ | ❏ | ❏ |
| b  Terry's father is angry about the letter. | ❏ | ❏ | ❏ |
| c  Terry wants to go to the party. | ❏ | ❏ | ❏ |
| d  Sue wasn't invited to the party. | ❏ | ❏ | ❏ |
| e  Jackie leaves next Saturday. | ❏ | ❏ | ❏ |
| f  Sue helps Terry with his History homework. | ❏ | ❏ | ❏ |
| g  Terry's father likes Sue. | ❏ | ❏ | ❏ |

— optional activity —

**5**  **Close your book. Listen again.**

# Useful expressions

**6** How do you say these expressions in your language?

I'm stuck.

And that's that.

It's no laughing matter.

I've been invited to a party.

I've had enough of your laziness.

Would you like a hand?

You're grounded.

Is that clear?

**7** a Work in groups of four. Each person takes one of the parts.

b Read the dialogue.

---
optional activity
---

## FOLLOW UP

**8** Complete the teacher's letter to Terry's parents.

### Hartfield Secondary School
West Hill, Hartfield, Bucks

Mr and Mrs Moore
20 Victoria Road
Hartfield HA9 4BJ

Dear Mr and Mrs Moore,

I'm writing to you about ............. . His work has been ............. recently. Here is an example of his answers to some History .............:
*Australia* ............. *discovered by Columbus.*
And here is an example from his ............. test. Question: *'Where is coffee .............?'* Answer: *'In supermarkets.'*
   I ............. know what is wrong with him, but it is now very serious. He ............. warned last week. This time I had to ............. to you. Please make an appointment to see me as soon as possible.

Yours sincerely

**K.Jones**

Mrs K. Jones

---

## The passive voice  ▶11.1–2

**1** a Look at these sentences.

You **were warned**.

The information **is checked** by the computer.

Your pocket money **will be stopped**.

The verbs in these sentences are in the **passive voice**.

b We make the passive voice with the verb 'to be' + a past participle. Identify these in the sentences above.

c Find more passive verbs in the story.

**2** a Look at this pair of sentences. Do they mean the same?

**Active**
The computer checks the information.

**Passive**
The information is checked by the computer.

We use the passive voice when the action is the most important thing.

b A passive sentence has these parts.

Subject   verb   (by + agent)

Find these parts in the sentences in Exercise 1a above.

**Note:** Not all sentences need an agent.

c Complete these sentences. Put the verbs in brackets into the passive voice.

The information ................. (receive) by the main

computer. It ................. (check). The results

................. (process). Then they

................. (store)

on the hard disk.

# Developing a film

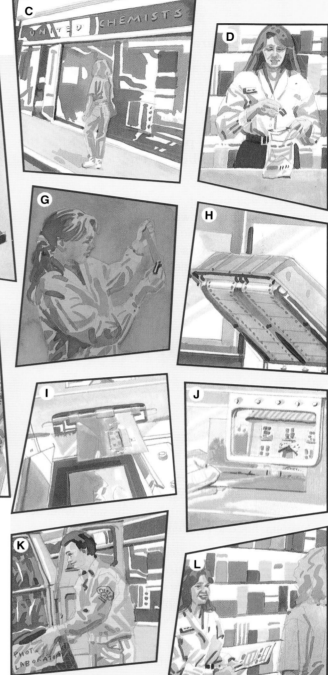

**3** **The pictures show the process for developing a film. Use these verbs to describe the process.**

take   remove   put   develop   send   collect
print   check   write

A  Photographs ........................ .

B  The film ...................... from the camera.

C  The film ...................... to the shop.

D  The film ...................... in an envelope.

E  The customer's name and address ...................
...................... on the envelope.

F  All the films ...................... to the laboratory.

G  The film ...................... from the cassette.

H  The film ...................... .

I  The film ...................... .

J  The photographs ...................... .

K  The photographs ...................... back to
the shop.

L  The photographs ...................... .

---

— optional activity —

**FOLLOW UP**

**4** **Look at the sentences in Exercise 3. Say who (or what) each stage of work is done by. Use these words.**

customer   shop assistant   printer
laboratory assistant   developing machine

Example
*Photographs are taken by the customer.*

## READING

**1** **Look at the pictures and the title.**

**a** What is the text about?

**b** Who are the people in the pictures. If you don't know, find their names in the text.

**2** **Look at this list of paragraph topics. Read the text quickly. Number the topics in the correct order.**

types of electric guitar
how an electric guitar works
the future of the electric guitar
the advantages and disadvantages of the guitar
the importance of the electric guitar
the first electric guitar

A

# The twentieth century's instrument

Think of rock music – anything from Elvis Presley and the Beatles to Guns 'n' Roses – and you will think of one musical instrument – the electric guitar. Rock music was created by the electric guitar.

The ordinary acoustic guitar has been played for centuries. It's easy to play. It's light and easy to carry. You can play it and sing at the same time. But the guitar has one problem. It isn't very loud.

This problem was solved in 1931 when the first electric guitar was produced in the USA by Adolph Rickenbacker. It was very simple and it didn't look very exciting. In fact, people called it 'the electric frying pan'. But popular music was revolutionized by this simple instrument.

In an electric guitar small microphones, or pickups, are placed under the strings. These pickups are connected to an amplifier and a speaker. There are controls for volume and tone on the guitar and on the amplifier. With modern electronics one guitar can be louder than a whole orchestra.

Today millions of electric guitars are sold around the world. The two most popular types were both developed in the 1950s and they have changed very little since then. The Les Paul is made by the Gibson guitar company and it is greatly loved by heavy metal guitarists like Slash of Guns 'n' Roses. But the most popular guitar of all is the Stratocaster. It is made by Fender and has been played by many famous rock guitarists including Jimi Hendrix, Keith Richards of the Rolling Stones and Eric Clapton.

Until the 1980s more guitars were sold in the USA than any other instrument. Since then, however, the guitar has been overtaken by the electronic keyboard, and in the future more and more music will be produced by computers. But the electric guitar won't be replaced. Keyboards and computers are all right in the recording studio, but on stage they can't compete with the raw energy of the guitar. Stratocasters and Les Pauls will be seen and heard on the rock stage into the next century and beyond.

**3** **Read the text more carefully. Say whether these statements are Right or Wrong according to the text.**

**a** A normal guitar is called an acoustic guitar.

**b** Guitars are difficult to play.

**c** The first electric guitar was produced in the 1930s.

**d** The first electric guitar was called a Stratocaster.

**e** In an electric guitar the strings are connected to the speaker.

**f** Slash plays a Les Paul.

**g** The Stratocaster is made by the Gibson guitar company.

**h** A lot of modern music is played on electronic keyboards.

**i** Electric guitars won't be used in the future.

B

C

## Tenses in the passive ►11.1

 **a** Complete these sentences from the text.

1 Rock music ..................... by the electric guitar.

2 The ordinary acoustic guitar ..................... for centuries.

3 Today millions of electric guitars ..................... around the world.

4 More and more music ..................... . by computers.

**b** What tense is the verb in each sentence?

**c** A passive verb has two parts, the verb 'to be' and the past participle. Which part shows the tense?

**d** Find examples of each tense in the text.

**e** Look at your answers to exercise 4b. What does the text say about the items? Use these verbs in the passive:

create   play   develop   make   replace
produce   invent   call

Examples
*The electric guitar was invented by Adolph Rickenbacker.*
*The electric guitar won't be replaced by keyboards.*

### W O R D   W O R K

 **a** Find all the words in the text connected with music.

**b** Can you add any more words?

---

 **a** Look at the pictures. Name the three types of guitar that you can see.

**b** Connect the items in column A and column B. Some may be connected to more than one.

| A | B |
|---|---|
| | Fender |
| | heavy metal guitarists |
| the electric guitar | the electric guitar |
| the Stratocaster | for centuries |
| the Les Paul | keyboards |
| rock music | Adolph Rickenbacker |
| the acoustic guitar | Slash |
| the first electric guitar | Gibson |
| | the electric frying pan |
| | Eric Clapton |

--- optional activities ---

 **Discuss these questions.**

**a** What musical instruments do people in your class play? Why did they choose them? What kind of music do they play?

**b** What advantages and disadvantages does the electric guitar have? Think about other instruments. What advantages and disadvantages do they have?

**c** What does the writer think about the future of the electric guitar? Do you agree?

**FOLLOW UP**

 Write your answers to exercise 5e. Write ten sentences.

# LISTENING

## THE TOP 40

 **1** **Read the short passage below. What programme is it about?**

Every Sunday afternoon at five o'clock the new singles chart is released on Radio 1's Top 40 programme. Radios in Britain and Europe are switched on to hear the latest news about pop music. The Top 40 is Europe's most popular programme. How is the chart produced?

**2** **The diagram shows how the Top 40 programme is made. Some of the stages are missing. What do you think the missing stages are?**

 **3** ▣ **Listen and complete the diagram.**

**4** **Listen again and find the answers to these questions.**

a How many records are released each week in Britain?

b How often is information sent to the central computer?

c How much information isn't used? Why not?

d Examples of different charts are given. What are they?

e How many record sales are needed to make a Number 1?

| W | O | R | D |  | W | O | R | K |
|---|---|---|---|---|---|---|---|---|

 **5** a **Write down all the words you heard that are connected with:**

- pop music • computers

b **Listen again. Can you add any more words to your list?**

---

records are recorded → **A**

each record is given a code number → **B**

records are bought → **C**

the information is sent to the main computer

**D** → 20% of the information is not used

the chart is produced and sent to the radio station

**E**

the programme is broadcast

---

*optional activity*

## FOLLOW UP

**6** **Complete this text with the correct form of the verbs in brackets.**

First, records are recorded. When they ..................... (release) each record ..................... (give) a code number. Then copies of the records ..................... (send) to shops. When records ..................... (buy), their code numbers ..................... (record) in the shop's computer. Then this information ..................... (send) to the central computer. The information ..................... (sort) and the Top 40 chart ..................... (produce). Then the chart ..................... (send) to the radio station and the programme ..................... (write) by the producer and the DJ. Finally the programme ..................... (broadcast) on Sunday afternoon.

# INTERACTION

## At the shops

**1 a** Here are the parts of two shopping dialogues. They are in the correct order, but they are mixed up. Write A or B next to each part.

**A** Have you got 'Can't Forget' by Yo Yo Rah, please?
**B** My watch isn't working. I think it needs a new battery.

❏ Just a minute I'll have a look in the catalogue. Is it a single or an album?

❏ An album.

❏ Hmm. Yes. Shall I put a new battery in for you?

❏ Ah yes. Here it is, but we haven't got it in stock.

❏ Yes, please.

❏ There you are. It's OK now.

❏ Can I order it?

❏ Certainly. What name is it, please?

❏ Thank you. How much is that?

❏ Collins. Sam Collins.

❏ £3.50 please.

❏ Here you are.

❏ OK. It will be about three days.

❏ Thank you. That's £1.50 change.

**b** Add a beginning and an ending to each dialogue.

**2 a**  Listen and check your dialogues.

**b** Practise the dialogues with a partner.

**3** Make new dialogues. Use these cues.

1 film for camera/ size?/ 35 mm (mill)/ exposures/ 36

2 radio needs new batteries/ size?/ triple A/ how many?/ 4

3 (your favourite record)/ CD or cassette/ CD/ only cassette/ order CD in two days

4 videotapes/ vhs/ how long?/ 3 hours/ how many?/ 2

— optional activity —

**FOLLOW UP**

**4** Write two of your dialogues from Exercise 4.

► Pronunciation: page 100

# PROJECT

## Planning and research

**1** For this project you must find some information. Before you begin, look at the six sections of the project in Exercise 2b below and consider these questions.

**a** What information will you need?

**b** What illustrations will be useful?

**c** Where will you find the information and illustrations?

**d** How will you present the project?

## Communication

**2** Find out and write about a form of communication that has revolutionized people's lives.

**a** Here are some possible ideas:

the car, the aeroplane, the rocket, computers, the radio, the telephone

Can you think of any more?

**b** Your project should have these five sections Find these sections in the text on p 90.

the importance of the form of communication
the situation before it was invented
its history and development
how it works
its uses today
possible future developments

**Learning diary** 11

What have you learnt in this unit?

**A** Do the self-check in the Workbook. Check any grammar problems in the reference section on pages 101–107.

**B** Look at the ways of revising that you discussed on page 85. Have you used any of them? How have they helped you?

Complete your learning diary.

# 12 revision

**tenses**
**reading skills**
**listening skills**

## *The jacket*

**▼1** **Look at the picture story**

**a** What is happening in each picture?

**b** Choose the correct alternative from each of these pairs to complete the story.

- 'm liking/like
- went out/'s gone out
- borrow/lend
- danced/were dancing
- bought/have bought
- doesn't know/won't know
- like/likes
- cold/hot
- needn't/mustn't
- any/ some

- that's that/I'm stuck
- has invited/has been invited
- Would you like/Do you like
- wear/'ll wear
- have you had/you have had
- better/worse
- took/was taking
- has stolen/has been stolen

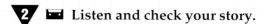
**▼2** 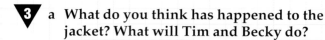 **Listen and check your story.**

**▼3** **a** What do you think has happened to the jacket? What will Tim and Becky do?

**b** 🔲 **Listen and find out what happens.**

─ optional activities ─

**▼4** **What do you think of Tim, Ben, and Becky? Were they right to do what they did? Why?**

**FOLLOW UP**

**▼5** **Work in groups of three. Role play the story.**

Tim ...................... to Becky's party. He wants to ............ his brother Ben's leather jacket.

**3** *Later*

I ............ your jacket, Tim. How long ............ it?

Oh… er.. I ............ it last week. ............ to dance, Becky?

**2**

Ben ............ . He ............ , if I ............ his jacket.

**1**

I said No and ............ .

Oh, come on, Ben. Becky really ............ leather jackets and I haven't got ............ money to get one.

*At the party*

**4**

Phew. It's ............ here.

Put your jacket on the chair. You ............ worry. It will be OK.

**5**

That's ............ .

**6**

Oh no. My jacket's gone. It ............ .

Oh, do you think someone ............ it while we ............?

94

**1** Jackie is going to America. What do you think will happen? Work in groups of five or six. Write a final episode, called: 'Goodbye, Jackie'.

**Your episode must:**

- have a part for every member of your group.
- be no more than two minutes long.
- contain at least five expressions from the Useful expressions sections.

optional activity

**2** **Act your episode.**

## VICTORIA ROAD

**3** 🔊 Listen to the final episode of Victoria Road. Compare it to yours. Is it the same in any way?

optional activity

### FOLLOW UP

**4** Jackie has been in America for three weeks. She writes a letter to her friends in Victoria Road. Imagine you are Jackie and write the letter. Describe:

- the journey
- your new home and friends
- what you have done

**and ask about people in Victoria Road.**

▶ Pronunciation: page 100

optional activity

 **5** Look at the song.

**a** What do you think the missing words are?

**b** 🔊 Listen and check your ideas.

### Dream Lover

*(written and recorded by Bobby Darin 1959)*

Every ........ I hope and pray
A dream lover ........ come my way,
A ........ to hold in my arms
And feel the ........ of her charms.

*Chorus*
*Because I ........ a girl*
*To call ........ own*
*I want a dream ........*
*So I don't have to ........ alone.*

Dream lover, ........ are you?
With a ........ oh so true,
And a ........ that I can hold,
To be near as I grow ........ .

Some day I don't ........ how,
I hope she'll ........ my plea
Some ........ I don't know how.
........ bring her love to me.

Dream lover, ........ then
I'll go to ........ and dream again.
That's the ........ thing to do
Till all my loving dreams come ........ .

# Learning *diary* 12

You've come to the end of this book. But it's not the end of learning English.

How do you feel about the things that you have learnt? Look back at your learning diaries in the book. Write down:

- 3 things that you know well now.
- 3 things that you are still not sure about.
- 3 things that you really enjoyed.
- 3 things that you didn't like much.

# PRONUNCIATION PRACTICE

## Introduction
### Phonetic alphabet revision

 **1** a  **These are the vowel sounds of English.**

| | | | |
|---|---|---|---|
| /iː/ | need | /juː/ | comp**u**ter |
| /ɪ/ | did | /ɜː/ | work |
| /e/ | ten | /ə/ | und**er** |
| /æ/ | cat | /eɪ/ | day |
| /ɑː/ | car | /aɪ/ | nine |
| /ʌ/ | run | /ɔɪ/ | boy |
| /ɒ/ | not | /aʊ/ | how |
| /ɔː/ | four | /əʊ/ | go |
| /ʊ/ | book | /eə/ | there |
| /uː/ | Sue | /ɪə/ | here |

b **Write one more word for each sound.**

c **Match the sounds to the correct word.**

Example
**A** /ɜː/ = *bird*.

| | | |
|---|---|---|
| **A** | /ɜː/ | come |
| **B** | /uː/ | watch |
| **C** | /aɪ/ | bird |
| **D** | /iː/ | can't |
| **E** | /ʌ/ | room |
| **F** | /əʊ/ | walk |
| **G** | /juː/ | night |
| **H** | /ɒ/ | sleep |
| **I** | /ɔː/ | new |
| **J** | /ɑː/ | don't |

d **Complete these words with the correct symbol:**

| | | | |
|---|---|---|---|
| /m......d/ | made | /sn ......../ | snow |
| /w ......z/ | was | /s ........d/ | said |
| /br ......t/ | brought | /f .......m/ | farm |
| /sk ......l/ | school | /j ........ / | year |

## Unit 1
### /z/, /ɪz/

 **1** a **Read these pairs of sentences.**

| | |
|---|---|
| I live here. | I wash the car. |
| Sue lives here. | Casey washes the car. |

**What do you notice about 'washes'?**

b **Copy this chart.**

| | /z/ | /ɪz/ |
|---|---|---|
| goes | | |
| watches | | |
| fetches | | |
| leaves | | |
| washes | | |
| plays | | |
| lives | | |
| closes | | |
| does | | |
| changes | | |
| passes | | |

c **Listen. Tick the correct column in your chart.**

d **Complete this rule.**

> **After .........., .........., .........., and ..........,**
> **-es is pronounced /ɪz/.**

### Syllable stress

 **2** **In words with two syllables, one syllable is usually stressed more than the other one.**

Examples
•bedroom   gui•tar

a **Look at these words. Which syllable has the stress?**

| | | | |
|---|---|---|---|
| bedroom | nothing | morning | breakfast |
| guitar | correct | matter | swimming |
| England | compare | thirty | dinner |
| housework | birthday | picture | around |
| problem | relax | repeat | quickly |

b **Listen and check your ideas.**

c **Which syllable usually has the stress?**

d **Listen again and repeat.**

# Unit 2

## -ed endings

**1** a  **Listen. What do you notice about the -ed?**

The car start**ed**.
The car stopp**ed**.

b **Put these words in the correct box.**

| | | | |
|---|---|---|---|
| played | stayed | painted | decided |
| recorded | wanted | visited | opened |
| died | needed | collected | saved |
| joined | received | lived | waited |

*started*

*stopped*

c  **Listen and check your answers.**

d **When do you pronounce the -ed? Make a rule.**

> You pronounce the -ed when the letter
> before the -ed is a .......... or a .......... .

## Sentence stress

**2** **In a sentence not all of the syllables are stressed equally.**

Examples
What did you do?
We painted my room.

a **Where is the stress in these sentences?**

A I'm going to the shops.
B Do you want to come?
C She's only kidding.
D I'm fed up with this.
E I phoned you yesterday morning.
F Were you ill on Saturday?
G What's the matter with Terry?
H I think he fancies Sue.

b  **Listen and check your ideas.**

c **Listen again and repeat.**

# Unit 3

## /ɪ/, /ɪ:/

**1** a **Look at these pairs of words.**

| | | | | | |
|---|---|---|---|---|---|
| A | hill | he'll | G | slip | sleep |
| B | chip | cheap | H | sit | seat |
| C | this | these | I | it | eat |
| D | bit | beat | J | fit | feet |
| E | will | wheel | K | live | leave |
| F | fill | feel | L | bin | been |

b  **Listen. You will hear one word from each pair. Which word do you hear?**

c **Listen again and repeat.**

## Weak vowels

**2** **When we speak, we change some vowels to /ə/. This is a weak and unstressed sound.**

Examples
/tə/
We went to New York.
/kən/
We can play tennis.

a **Look at these sentences. Which vowels change to an /ə/ sound?**

Example
/ə/
There are two cafes in this town.
'a' in 'are' changes.

A The bus stop's in front of the school.
B You can buy sweets in that shop.
C Where does he live?
D Is there a pub in this street?
E What are you doing?
F I'm going to the shop.
G John was in France on Tuesday.
H They're Vince and Sue.
I Carmen's from Spain.

b  **Listen and check your ideas.**

c **Listen again and repeat.**

# Unit 4
## Phonetic alphabet revision

**▼1** a  **These are the consonant sounds of English.**

| | | | | |
|---|---|---|---|---|
| /d/ | **d**og | /ð/ | **th**is | |
| /t/ | **t**o | /θ/ | four**th** | |
| /b/ | **b**ig | /s/ | **s**ix | |
| /p/ | **p**en | /z/ | **z**oo | |
| /g/ | **g**ood | /ŋ/ | si**ng** | |
| /k/ | **c**ome | /j/ | **y**esterday | |
| /ʃ/ | **sh**e | /h/ | **h**ow | |
| /tʃ/ | **r**i**ch** | /m/ | **m**an | |
| /ʒ/ | lei**s**ure | /n/ | **n**o | |
| /dʒ/ | **j**acket | /l/ | **l**eg | |
| /f/ | **f**rom | /r/ | **r**ed | |
| /v/ | **v**ery | /w/ | **w**et | |

b **Write one more word for each sound.**

c **Complete these words with the correct symbol.**

| | | | |
|---|---|---|---|
| /....... iːp/ | cheap | /....... ʌn/ | one |
| /....... æmrə/ | camera | /....... iːz/ | these |
| /tʃeɪn ......./ | change | /....... es/ | yes |
| /....... ɔː/ | sure | /bɑː: ......./ | bath |
| /....... æfeɪ/ | cafe | /pliː: ......./ | please |

# Unit 5
## /r/

**▼1** a  **Listen. Can you hear the /r/?**

They t**R**avelled a**R**ound the wo**R**ld in a ca**R**.

b **Put these words in Africa if we say the 'r'
or Antarctica if we don't say the 'r'.**

| | | | |
|---|---|---|---|
| year | breakfast | brother | sport |
| terrible | dinner | picture | equator |
| America | travel | north | morning |
| over | bird | Arctic | strong |

| Africa | Antarctica |
|---|---|
| | |

c  **Listen and check your answers.**

## Syllable stress

**▼2** **In three-syllable words we usually stress
only one syllable.**

Examples
lib•rary  Antar•ctic  maga•zine

a **Which syllable has the stress?**

| | |
|---|---|
| newsagent's | excellent |
| direction | secondary |
| afternoon | equator |
| avenue | yesterday |
| Africa | forever |
| observant | Atlantic |
| computer | tomorrow |
| understand | serious |
| animal | cigarette |
| excited | eleven |

b  **Listen and check your ideas.**

c **Listen again and repeat.**

d **Where are the /ə/ sounds?**

# Unit 6
## /h/

**▼1**  **Listen. If you hear the /h/ sound, repeat
the word. If you don't hear /h/, stay silent.**

## Strong and weak forms

**▼2** **Auxiliary verbs, such as 'be', 'can', 'have', and
'do', have strong and weak forms.**

Example
/ə/
Are you going to the shops?
　　　/ɑː/
Yes, we are.

 **Listen and repeat.**

a Do they like jazz?
Yes, they do.

b Does she live here now?
Yes, she does.

c Have you got a pen?
Yes, I have.

d Were they at the party?
Yes, they were.

e I can swim 200 metres.
Can you swim 300 metres?

# Unit 7
## /ʃ/, /tʃ/

 **a** **Look at these pairs of words.**

| | | | | | |
|---|---|---|---|---|---|
| **A** | ship | chip | **E** | wash | watch |
| **B** | shoe | chew | **F** | sheep | cheap |
| **C** | wish | which | **G** | shop | chop |
| **D** | cash | catch | | | |

**b**  **Listen. You will hear one word from each pair. Which word do you hear?**

**c** **Listen again and repeat.**

## Intonation

**2** **a** **There are two important intonation patterns.**

The intonation rises at the end of the sentence. ↗
The intonation falls at the end of the sentence. ↘

**Match these kinds of sentences to the correct pattern.**

**A** *Wh-* questions: Where do you live?
**B** 'Yes/No' questions: Are you from Portugal?
**C** Statements: I like rock music.

**b**  **Listen and check your ideas.**

**A** Can you play the guitar?
Yes, I can.
**B** Where can we play tennis round here?
You can play in the park.
**C** What was Kam doing?
She was putting things on the shelves.
**D** Was she watching Terry?
Yes, she was.
**E** When were they in Spain?
They were there in August.
**F** Were they in Barcelona?
Yes, they were.

**c** **Listen again and repeat.**

**d** **Say the dialogues with a partner.**

# Unit 8
## A secret message

**1** **What is the message? Write it in words.**

/juː wɪl əskeɪp ət kwɔːtə tə θriː/

/ɒn θɜːzdeɪ ðə naɪnθ əv dʒuːlaɪ/

/weɪt fɔːr ə wʊmən wɪð lɒŋ braʊn heə/

/ʃiː wɪl kʌm ɪn ə jeləʊ kɑː/

# Unit 9
## Vowel sounds

 **Find the odd one out.**

**a** **Look at the groups of three words. Two of the three words have the same vowel sound. Which is the odd one out?**

| | | | |
|---|---|---|---|
| **A** | have | save | brave |
| **B** | park | car | pack |
| **C** | done | gone | son |
| **D** | know | now | no |
| **E** | post | lost | cost |
| **F** | don't | front | won't |
| **G** | can | aren't | car |
| **H** | here | where | there |
| **I** | eat | feet | great |
| **J** | put | look | luck |

**b**  **Listen and check your ideas.**

**c** **Listen again and repeat.**

## Intonation

**2** **a** **Look.**

Have you ever spoken to a tourist?

I've got an English penfriend.

**b**  **Listen. Is it a question or a statement?**

**c** **Listen again and repeat.**

# Unit 10
## /ɪz/ plural endings

**1** **a**  **Listen and give the plural.**

Example
glass → glasses   hamburger → hamburgers

watch   bottle   sausage   tin   tomato   brush
badge   lemon   potato   orange   slice

**b** **When do we pronounce the plural endings /ɪz/?**

## Emphatic stress

 We use emphatic stress to contradict or correct something.

Examples
*What's her name?*
***His** name's Greg.*

*Is the book on the desk?*
*No, it's on the **table**.*

**When we use emphatic stress, we use the strong form of the word, not the weak form.**

/ə/
**A** I was at the party. Why weren't you there?
/wɒz/
**B** I *was* at the party.

a **Look at these dialogues. Which word has the emphatic stress?**

> **A** Is this Jackie's camera?
> No, it's Greg's camera.
> **B** Is it September 9th today?
> No, it's September 10th.
> **C** Are you sixteen?
> No, I'm fifteen.
> **D** Why haven't you done your homework?
> I have done it.
> **E** Is Sue going to the shops?
> She's already at the shops.
> **F** Is the train at ten to nine?
> No, it's at ten past nine.

b  **Listen and check your ideas.**

c **Listen again and repeat.**

# Unit 11
## -ea

 **The letters *-ea* can be pronounced in several different ways.**

a **Look at the words below. How are these words pronounced? Copy the chart and put the words in the right columns.**

weather  leave  clear  earth  reach  bread
meat  dead  leather  disappear  seat  ear
cream  meal  heavy  learn

| /e/ | /iː/ | /ɪə/ | /ɜː/ |
|---------|-------|-------|-------|
| weather | leave | clear | earth |

b  **Listen and check your ideas.**

c **Listen again and repeat.**

## Sentence stress

 **English is a stress-timed language. This means that sentences with the same number of stresses will take the same amount of time, regardless of how many syllables they have. Syllables are made longer or shorter to fit the rhythm.**

a **Look at this example and listen.**

Example
•           •           •
*A letter will be sent to your parents.*

b **The time between the stresses is the same. But how many syllables are there between the first and second stresses? How many syllables are there between the second and third stresses?**

c  **Listen.**

•          •
Come on, John
•         •
It's time to go.
•           •         •
It's quarter past seven.
•      •
Yes, I know.
•         •       •
What are you doing?
•        •
I'm looking for my keys.
•                   •         •
I don't know where I left them.
•        •
Hurry up, please.

d **Listen again and repeat. Keep the rhythm.**

# Unit 12
## A secret message

 **What is the message? Write it in words.**

/tɪm wɒntɪd tə bɑrəʊ benz leðə dʒækɪt bʌt hiː sed nəʊ/

100

# GRAMMAR REFERENCE

## I.1 The verb 'to be': statements

| I | am<br>'m<br>am not<br>'m not | from New York. |
|---|---|---|
| He<br>She<br>(It) | is<br>'s<br>is not<br>isn't | sixteen. |
| We<br>You<br>They | are<br>'re<br>are not<br>aren't | in the kitchen.<br>late. |

We usually use the long form when we write. We use the short form when we speak. After 'this', we always use the long form.

We can use the verb 'to be' to talk about temporary and permanent states.

Examples
*He is in the kitchen. (temporary)*
*He is my brother. (permanent)*

## I.2 The verb 'to be': questions

To make questions we put the verb in front of the subject.

Examples
*Is she in the kitchen? Yes, she is.*
*Are you sixteen? No, I'm not.*

## I.3 Possessive adjectives

| I | my | it | its |
|---|---|---|---|
| you | your | we | our |
| he | his | they | their |
| she | her | | |

Possessive adjectives do not change with plural nouns.

The possessive adjective we use depends on who (or what) possesses something, not what they possess. We use 'his' for a boy or a man, and 'her' for a girl or a woman.

Examples
*my shoe*            *her house (Kamala's house)*
*my shoes*          *his house (Vince's house)*
*our friend*          *their son*
*our friends*        *their sons*

## I.4 have/has got: statements

| I<br>You<br>We<br>They | have<br>'ve<br>have not<br>haven't | got | a computer<br>two sisters. |
|---|---|---|---|
| He<br>She<br>(It) | has<br>'s<br>has not<br>hasn't | | a blue car |

Note: After words ending in /s/, /z/, /tʃ/, /ʃ/, /dʒ/ we do not normally use the short form of 'has'. We use the full form.

Examples
*Vince has got a sister.*
*The village has got a new leisure complex.*

## I.5 have/has got: questions and answers

To make questions, we put 'have' or 'has' in front of the subject. In quick answers we do not use 'got'.

Examples
*Have you got a computer? Yes, I have.*
*Has he got a car? No, he hasn't.*

## 1.1 Telling the time

When the number of minutes can be divided by five, we don't normally say 'minutes'. For all other times, we must put in the word 'minutes'. We can also give times in digital form.

Examples
*five past five    BUT seventeen minutes past four*
*3.30    three thirty*

## 1.2 The present simple tense: statements

| I<br>You<br>We<br>They | play<br>like | tennis. |
|---|---|---|
| He<br>She<br>(It) | plays<br>likes | |

In the third person singular we add -s to the infinitive.

There are some exceptions. When the verb ends in -ss, -sh, -ch, or -o, we add -es. When the verb ends in -y, we change the -y to -ies.

Examples
*miss → misses, finish → finishes, catch → catches, go → goes, hurry → hurries*

## 1.3 The present simple tense: negative statements

| I You We They | do not don't | | like play | tennis. |
|---|---|---|---|---|
| He She (It) | does not doesn't | | | |

The short form of 'do not' is 'don't'.
The short form of 'does not' is 'doesn't'.

## 1.4 The present simple tense: questions and answers

To make questions we use:
do or does + subject + infinitive.

Examples
*Do you like football? Yes I do.*
*Does he play tennis? No, he doesn't.*

Note: In negatives and questions we use the stem form, ('like', 'play') of the verb. There is no -s on the verb in the third person.

Examples
*She doesn't like him. NOT She doesn't likes him.*
*Does he play football? NOT Does he plays football?*

## 1.5 The present simple tense: use

We use the present simple tense to:
– describe regular events or permanent states.
– talk about general truths.

Examples
*I get up at half past five (every day).*
*She likes pop music.*
*Lions live in Africa.*

## 1.6 this/these, that/those

We use 'this/that' with singular nouns and 'these/those' with plural nouns.

Examples
*this book/these books    that child/those children*

We use 'this/these' for things that are near us. We use 'that/those' for things that are further away.

We pronounce 'this' /ðɪs/ and 'these' /ðiːz/.

## 1.7 Plurals

To make most plurals we add -s to the noun.

Examples
*a dog/two dogs    one girl/three girls*

With words ending in *-ss, -ch, -sh* or *-o*, we add *-es*.

Examples
*a watch → two watches    a tomato → two tomatoes*

With plurals ending in /tʃ/, /ʃ/, /dʒ/, /s/, and /z/, we pronounce the plural ending /ɪz/.

Examples
*watches* /wɒtʃɪz/    *badges* /bædʒɪz/

A few plurals are irregular.

## 1.8 Prepositions of time: in/at/on

We use 'in' for years, months and parts of the day, but we say 'at' night.

Examples
*in 1990    in February    in the afternoon*
*NOT of the afternoon*

We use 'on' for days and dates. We do not normally use the article with days of the week.

Examples
*on Monday            on 9 September 1978*
*on Christmas Day     on my birthday*

We do not write the article with dates, but we do say it when we speak.

Example
*We write: on 4th May 1996, or, on 4 May 1996.*
*We say: on the fourth of May 1996.*

We use 'at' for times of the day and occasions with more than one day.

Examples
*at nine o'clock     at the weekend*
*at 10.15            at Christmas*

## 2.1 The past simple tense: the verb 'to be', statements

| I He She (It) | was was not wasn't | at school | |
|---|---|---|---|
| | | | yesterday. |
| We You They | were were not weren't | ill | |

## 2.2 The past simple tense: the verb 'to be', questions and answers

To make questions we put 'was' or 'were' in front of the subject.

Examples
*Was she at school yesterday? Yes, she was.*
*Were they here last week? No, they weren't.*

## 2.3 The past simple tense: regular verbs

To make the past simple tense we add -*ed* to the stem form of the verb. The past simple tense is the same for all persons.

Examples
watch        *She watched television last night.*
happen       *It happened yesterday.*

### Spelling exceptions

When the verb ends in -*e*, we add -*d*.

When the verb ends in a consonant + *y*, we remove the -*y* and add -*ied*.

When the verb ends in a short vowel and a single consonant, we normally double the consonant and add -*ed*.

Examples
*live→lived   carry→carried   stop→stopped*

## 2.4 The past simple tense: irregular verbs

Many common verbs have an irregular past form. See the list on page 111. The irregular form is the same for all persons.

Examples
give         *I gave him the coat.*
throw        *He threw it into the lake.*

## 2.5 The past simple tense: negatives, questions and answers

To make negatives we use:
subject + didn't + infinitive.

Example
*She didn't go to London.*

To make questions we use:
did + subject + infinitive.

Example
*Did you like the film? Yes, I did.*

Note: In negatives and questions we use the stem form of the verb.

Example
*She didn't like the film. NOT ~~She didn't liked the film.~~*

## 2.6 Prepositions of place

We use 'to' to show movement.

Example
*She's going to the shops.* (But note: *She's going home.*)
We use 'in' when there is no movement; with towns, cities, countries and parts of a house. We usually use 'in' after 'live' and 'work'.

Examples
*She's in Rome.    He's in the bathroom.*
*She lives in a big house.    He works in a bank.*

We use 'at' when there is no movement. We use 'at' for places where you do something.

Examples
*at school    at the restaurant*

## 3.1 The present continuous tense

We make the present continuous tense with the verb 'to be' and the -*ing* form of the verb (the present participle).

Examples
*I'm reading a book.    She's having a shower.*
*We're waiting for the bus.*

To make negative statements we use the negative form of the verb 'to be'.

Examples
*I'm not reading a book.    She isn't having a shower.    We aren't waiting for the bus.*

## 3.2 The present continuous tense: questions and answers

To make questions we put the verb 'to be' in front of the subject. The main verb comes after the subject.

Examples
*Is he watching TV? Yes, he is.*
*Are you using the phone? No, I'm not.*

## 3.3 The present continuous tense: spelling rules

The basic rule is: add -*ing* to the infinitive.

Examples
*wash → washing   read → reading*

For verbs that end in -*e*, we remove the -*e* and add -*ing*. For verbs with a short vowel and only one consonant, we usually double the consonant and add -*ing*.

Examples
*drive → driving   use → using*
*swim → swimming   sit → sitting*

## 3.4 The present continuous tense and the present simple tense

We use the present continuous tense to say what is happening at the moment.

Examples
*We're waiting for the bus at the moment.*
*Where's Terry? He's having a shower.*

We use the present simple tense to describe a regular event.

Example
*We usually meet at the leisure centre, but today we're meeting at Sue's house.*

Note: 'What do you do?' does NOT mean 'What are you doing (now)?'

Example
*What do you do? I'm an engineer   NOT I'm eating.*

## 3.5 there is/there are

| There | is 's | a book a computer | on the table. |
| | are | two computers five books | |

We use 'there is/are' to express that something exists. We use 'there is' with singular nouns and 'there are' with plural nouns.
Note: There is no short form for 'there are'.

To make questions we put 'is' or 'are' in front of 'there'.

Example
*How many students are there in your class?*

Note: 'people' takes the plural of the verb.

## 5.1 The future simple tense ('will'): positive and negative statements

One way to talk about the future is to use the future simple tense with 'will'. To make the future simple tense we put 'will' or -'ll in front of the verb. For the negative we put 'will not' or 'won't' in front of the infinitive.

| I He She (It) | will 'll | telephone Selin. help Sue. |
| We You They | will not won't | be away for three weeks. wait. |

With 'I' and 'we' we can also say 'shall/shan't'. The short form of 'shall' is also -'ll.

Examples
*We shall meet at two o'clock.   I shan't go home.*

## 5.2 The future simple tense ('will'): questions and answers

To make questions in the future, we put 'will' in front of the subject.

Example
*Will you need any help? Yes, I will.*

With 'I' and 'We' you can use 'shall'. This usually means a suggestion or that something is not certain.

Examples
*Shall we go out?   What shall I wear?*

## 5.3 The future simple tense: use

We use the future with 'will' to make predictions or general statements about the future.

Examples
*I won't be here next week.    The weather will be fine.*

## 5.4 First conditionals ('if' clauses)

First conditionals predict the effects of a real or probable action or event.

Example
*If you lie in the sun too long, you'll get sunburnt.*

We use the present simple tense in the 'if' clause and the future with 'will' in the main clause.

Example
*If it rains, we won't go out.*
'if' clause    main clause

We use the same form with time clauses.

Example
*We'll wait here until he arrives.*
main clause    time clause

## 5.5 must, mustn't, needn't

| I He She (It) We You They | must mustn't needn't | use the computer. leave. go now. |

'Mustn't' is the short form of 'must not'. 'Must' means it is compulsory or necessary. 'Needn't' means it is not compulsory or necessary. 'Mustn't' means it is not allowed or 'Don't do it'.

Example
*On a plane, you must wear a seat belt when the plane is taking off. But you needn't wear it for the whole flight. You mustn't smoke in the 'No smoking' section.*

## 6.1 The past continuous tense: positive and negative statements

| I<br>He<br>She<br>(It) | was<br>was not<br>wasn't | going to the shops.<br><br>watching TV. |
| We<br>You<br>They | were<br>were not<br>weren't | waiting for a bus. |

Note: there is no short form of the positive, only of the negative.

## 6.2 The past continuous tense: questions and answers

To make questions in the past continuous tense we put 'was' or 'were' in front of the subject.

> Examples
> *Was she wearing a jacket? Yes, she was.*
> *Were they going to the cinema? No, they weren't.*

## 6.3 The past continuous tense: use

The past continuous tense describes a continuous or incomplete activity in the past.

We often use it with the past simple tense. The past continuous sets the scene. The past simple says what happened. The clauses are usually joined by 'while', 'as', or 'when'.

> Examples
> *While I was having lunch, the telephone rang.*
> *As she was going downstairs, she fell.*

Compare these two sentences.

> *While I was having lunch, the telephone rang.*
> *When I heard the phone, I went to answer it.*

The first sentence has a past continuous tense to set the scene and a past simple tense to say what happened. The second sentence has two past simple tenses. One action happened after the other.

## 6.4 Apostrophes

We use an apostrophe (') for two things, genitives and short forms.

> Examples
> Genitives:
> *Rebecca's tennis racket.    The girls' tennis club.*
> Short forms:
> *We'll go to Paris tomorrow.    I've got two brothers.*
> *Terry's in love.    Sue's got short hair.*

We must use the genitive with an apostrophe with proper names.

> Example
> *Kamala's friend    NOT ~~the friend of Kamala.~~*

We do not use apostrophes with a plural -s.

> Example
> *I've got two cats.    NOT ~~I've got two cat's.~~*

## 7.1 Comparatives and superlatives

To make the comparative of adjectives we add *-er* /ə/ to the adjective.
To make the superlative of adjectives we add *-est* /ɪst/ to the adjective.

> Example
> *short    shorter    the shortest*

### Exceptions

For adjectives that end in *-e*, we add *-r* or *-st*. For adjectives with a short vowel and only one consonant, we double the consonant and add *-er* or *-est*. For adjectives that end in *-y*, we remove the *-y* and add *-ier* or *-iest*.

> Examples
> *nice    nicer    the nicest*
> *wet    wetter    the wettest*
> *easy    easier    the easiest*

For adjectives with two or more syllables (where the second syllable is not *-y*), we do not add *-er* or *-est*. We put 'more' or 'most' in front of the adjective.

> Examples
> *modern    more modern    the most modern*
> *important    more important    the most important*

Note: Some two-syllable adjectives follow the basic rule. Unfortunately there is no rule for which adjectives do this.

> Example
> *clever    cleverer    the cleverest*

A few adjectives are completely irregular.

> Examples
> *good    better    the best*
> *bad    worse    the worst*
> *far    further    the furthest*

When we compare two things or people, we use the comparative and the word 'than'.

> Example
> *She's cleverer than her sister.*
> *NOT ~~She's cleverer that her sister.~~*
> *    ~~She's cleverer as her sister.~~*

## 7.2 Plurals of clothes

The names of some clothes are always plural.

Examples
*jeans   trousers   shorts*

These words take plural articles and verbs.

Examples
*These trousers are too short.*
*I need some new jeans. NOT I need a new jean.*

When we talk about a quantity of clothes, we must use 'pairs of' with words that are already plural.

Examples
*three T-shirts, two pairs of jeans, a pair of shoes.*

## 9.1 The present perfect tense: statements

| I<br>You<br>We<br>They | have<br>'ve<br>have not<br>haven't | bought a new shirt.<br><br>received the letter. |
|---|---|---|
| He<br>She<br>(It) | has<br>'s<br>has not<br>hasn't | had lunch.<br><br>been to America. |

Note: After words ending in /s/, /z/, /tʃ/, /ʃ/, or /dʒ/, we do not normally use the short form of 'has'. We use the full form.

Example
*Vince has not been to school today.*

## 9.2 The present perfect tense: questions

To make questions we put 'have' or 'has' in front of the subject.

Examples
*Have you written the letters? Yes, I have.*
*Has she been to America? No, she hasn't.*

## 9.3 The present perfect tense: form

We make the present perfect tense with the verb 'have/has' and the past participle of the verb.

To form regular past participles, we add -*ed* to the verb stem.

Examples
*wait → waited   stay → stayed*

This is the same as the regular past tense (see 2.3 for spelling rules).

A lot of common verbs have an irregular past participle. See the list on page 111.

Examples
*go → gone   write → written*

## 9.4 The present perfect tense: use

The present perfect links the past with the present. We use it in four ways:
– When we are interested in the present result of a past action.
– When the activity started in the past and still continues in the present. Note: We do not use the present tense in this context.
– When we are referring to a time that comes up to the present.
– When we talk about our experiences, but not *when* we did them.

Examples
*We've had our lunch. (We're not hungry now.)*
*I've lived here for two years. (I still live here now.)*
*NOT I live here for two years. or I am living here for two years.*
*Have you seen Jackie today? (It is still 'today'.)*
*I have travelled by plane many times.*

We use 'never' when we haven't done that thing or had that experience.

Example
*I've never travelled by plane.*

## 9.5 The present perfect tense and the past simple tense

Compare the uses of the present perfect in 9.4 with these uses of the past simple.

We use the past simple:
– When we are interested in the action or the time of the action, not the effect.

Examples
*I've seen that film. (So I know the story.)*
*I saw it last week. (The time of the activity.)*

– When the action finished in the past.

Examples
*I've lived in Warsaw for a year (I still live there.)*
*I lived in Warsaw for a year. (I don't live there now.)*

When there is a past time reference (e.g. in 1993, two days ago, last week), you must use the past simple tense, not the present perfect.

Example
*He went at 2 p.m.   NOT He has gone at 2 p.m.*

## 9.6 been/gone

'Be' and 'go' have a particular meaning in the present perfect tense.

Example
*She's gone to London. (She is still in London.)*
*She's been to London. (She has come back.)*

## 9.7 for/since

We often use 'for' and 'since' with the present perfect tense. We use 'for' with a period of time. We use 'since' with a point of time.

Examples
*I've lived here for two years.*
*I've lived here since 1991.*

## 9.8 Capital letters

We use capital letters for names; days and months; the beginning of a sentence; countries, nationalities and languages.

Examples
*Casey, August, Turkey, Portuguese*

## 10.1 Expressing quantity: some/any

'Some' and 'any' are the indefinite articles for plural nouns and uncountable nouns (see 10.2). We usually use 'some' with positive statements. We usually use 'any' with negative statements and questions.

Examples
*I need some new shoes.    We haven't got any bread.*
*Have you got any stamps?*

## 10.2 Expressing quantity: countable and uncountable nouns

Some nouns are countable. They have a singular and a plural form.

Example
*I had an egg for breakfast. I must buy some eggs.*

Some nouns are uncountable. They have no plural form. But they can't take the singular article 'a/an'. They use only 'some' or 'any'.

Examples
*I need some bread.    Have you got any money?*
*I've got some information for you.*
*NOT I've got some informations for you.*

These things are usually uncountable:

Drinks: *tea, beer, wine, water, coffee, milk*
Food which you only eat part of: *fish, bread, cheese, ham, meat*
Things which you only use part of: *toothpaste, soap, shampoo*
Materials: *paper, wood, wool, plastic*
Some general words: *information, music, money*

We use 'How many ...?' with countable nouns and 'How much ...?' with uncountable nouns.

Examples
*How many sandwiches do we need?*
*How much cheese have we got left?*

## 11.1 The passive voice: form

We make the passive voice with the verb 'to be' and a past participle.

Examples
*These watches are made in Switzerland.*
*English is spoken in many different countries.*

We can use the passive voice in any tense. To make different tenses we change the verb 'to be'.

Examples
*past: The jacket was stolen.*
*present perfect: The films have been developed.*
*present: The information is sent to the main computer.*
*future: A letter will be written to your parents.*

To make the negative of the passive voice, we use the negative of the verb 'to be'. To make questions we use the normal question form of the verb 'to be' in each tense.

Examples
*The jacket wasn't stolen.    Was the jacket stolen?*
*Sue wasn't grounded.    Was Terry grounded?*

## 11.2 The passive voice: use

The passive voice is very common in English. We use the passive voice when the action is more important than who or what did it, or when we don't know who did the action. If we want to show who or what does the action, we use 'by'.

Examples
*The code numbers are recorded.*
*The code numbers are recorded by the shop assistants.*

# WORDLIST

## INTRODUCTION

agency /'eɪdʒənsɪ/
angry /'æŋgrɪ/
annoyed /ə'nɔɪd/
Argentina /ɑ:dʒen'ti:nə/
brain /breɪn/
Brazil /brə'zɪl/
Come in! /kʌm 'ɪn/
Come on! /kʌm 'ɒn/
concentrate /'kɒnsəntreɪt/
flat /flæt/
fool /fu:l/
garden /'gɑ:dən/
grandma /'grændmɑ:/
grandpa /'grændpɑ:/
Hang on! /hæŋ 'ɒn/
Hurry up! /ˌhʌrɪ 'ʌp/
kitchen /'kɪtʃɪn/
letter /'letə/
mine (pron.) /maɪn/
mouth /maʊθ/
penfriend /'penfrend/
photograph /'fəʊtəgrɑ:f/
postcode /'pəʊstkəʊd/
rude /ru:d/
See you! /'si: ju:/
Ssh! /ʃ/
such a … /'sʌtʃ ə/
surname /'sɜ:neɪm/
That's a pity. /ˌðæts ə 'pɪtɪ/
worry /'wʌrɪ/

## UNIT 1   DAILY LIFE

about /ə'baʊt/
adult /'ædʌlt/
again /ə'gen/
all day /ɔ:l deɪ/
all the time /ˌɔ:l ðə 'taɪm/
amazing /ə'meɪzɪŋ/
around here /əˌraʊnd 'hɪə(r)/
asleep /ə'sli:p/
baby /'beɪbɪ/
bank /bæŋk/
bicycle /'baɪsɪkl/
bored /bɔ:d/
clean your teeth /ˌkli:n yɔ: 'ti:θ/
close (v.) /kləʊz/
cold /kəʊld/
community work /kə'mju:nɪtɪ wɜ:k/
cook /kʊk/
day /deɪ/
dig /dɪg/
dinner /'dɪnə/
dream /dri:m/
friendly /'frendlɪ/
funny /'fʌnɪ/
get dressed /get 'drest/
homework /'həʊmwɜ:k/
hospital /'hɒspɪtəl/
hour /'aʊə(r)/
housework /'haʊswɜ:k/

hungry /'hʌŋgrɪ/
iron (v.) /'aɪən/
language school /'læŋgwɪdʒ ˌsku:l/
launderette /lɔ:n'dret/
lazy /'leɪzɪ/
lesson /'lesən/
life /laɪf/
lunchtime /'lʌntʃtaɪm/
make your bed /ˌmeɪk yɔ: 'bed/
museum /mju:'zɪəm/
need (v.) /ni:d/
normal /'nɔ:məl/
nothing /'nʌθɪŋ/
other /'ʌðə(r)/
play the guitar /ˌpleɪ ðə gɪ'tɑ:/
post office /'pəʊst ˌɒfɪs/
problem /'prɒbləm/
pyjamas /pə'dʒɑ:məz/
remember /rɪ'membə(r)/
ride /raɪd/
robot /'rəʊbɒt/
shave /ʃeɪv/
shopping bag /'ʃɒpɪŋ bæg/
shower /'ʃaʊə/
sleep (n. and v.) /sli:p/
sleepwalk /'sli:pwɔ:k/
sleepwalker /'sli:pwɔ:kə/
snore /snɔ:(r)/
stay /steɪ/
suggest /sʌ'dʒest/
talk /tɔ:k/
teenager /'ti:neɪdʒə(r)/
teeth /ti:θ/
tennis /'tenɪs/
the same /ðə 'seɪm/
tidy /'taɪdɪ/
till /tɪl/
tired /'taɪəd/
too /tu:/
tourist /'tʊərɪst/
Wales /weɪlz/
walk /wɔ:k/
wash /wɒʃ/
wash up /ˌwɒʃ 'ʌp/
weather /'weðə(r)/
weekend /wi:'kend/
What's the matter? /ˌwɒts ðə 'mætə(r)/
What's the time …? /ˌwɒts ðə 'taɪm/
Why don't you …? /'waɪ dəʊnt ju:/
woke up /ˌwəʊk 'ʌp/
wrong /rɒŋ/
young /jʌŋ/

## UNIT 2   THE PAST

album /'ælbəm/
army /'ɑ:mɪ/
arrive /ə'raɪv/
autograph /'ɔ:təgrɑ:f/
be only kidding /bɪ ˌəʊnlɪ 'kɪdɪŋ/
because /bɪ'kɒz/
boss /bɒs/

busy /'bɪzɪ/
career /kə'rɪə(r)/
choir /'kwaɪə(r)/
church /tʃɜ:tʃ/
depressed /dɪ'prest/
died /daɪd/
disc jockey /'dɪsk 'dʒɒkɪ/
electronic /'elektrɒnɪk/
evaluation /ɪvælju:'eɪʃən/
fan club /'fæn klʌb/
fancy (v.) /'fænsɪ/
fantastic /fæn'tæstɪk/
fat /fæt/
fed up with /ˌfed 'ʌp wɪð/
feel ill /ˌfi:l 'ɪl/
felt ill /ˌfelt 'ɪl/
flu /flu:/
have a good laugh /ˌhæv ə ˌgʊd 'lɑ:f/
have a good time /ˌhæv ə ˌgʊd 'taɪm/
heart attack /'hɑ:t əˌtæk/
hit (record) /hɪt/
ill /ɪl/
jar /dʒɑ:(r)/
kids /kɪdz/
king /kɪŋ/
laugh /lɑ:f/
lay off (of) /leɪ ɒf (əv)/
liquor /'lɪkə/
listen to /'lɪsən tu:, tə/
lonely /'ləʊnlɪ/
machine /mə'ʃi:n/
magazine /mægə'zi:n/
manager /'mænɪdʒə(r)/
mansion /'mænʃən/
married /'mærɪd/
million /'mɪljən/
mirror /'mɪrə(r)/
never /'nevə(r)/
paint /peɪnt/
plate /pleɪt/
pop music /'pɒp ˌmju:zɪk/
poster /'pəʊstə(r)/
private /'praɪvət/
radio station /'reɪdɪəʊ ˌsteɪʃən/
recording studio /rɪ'kɔ:dɪŋ ˌstju:dɪəʊ/
rock and roll /ˌrɒk ənd 'rəʊl/
sang /sæŋ/
secretary /'sekrətrɪ/
sexy /'seksɪ/
show /ʃəʊ/
single /'sɪŋgəl/
statue /'stætʃu:/
strange /streɪndʒ/
stupid /'stju:pɪd/
sweatshirt /'swetʃɜ:t/
suede /sweɪd/
tease /ti:z/
teddy bear /'tedɪ ˌbeə(r)/
tell /tel/
What about …? /ˌwɒt ə'baʊt/
wild /waɪld/
wipe /waɪp/

## UNIT 3   PLACES

a lot /ə 'lɒt/
above /ə'bʌv/
actually /'æktʊəlɪ/
anything /'enɪθɪŋ/
at the end of /ət ðɪ 'end əv/
at the moment /ət ðə 'məʊmənt/
beat /bi:t/
behind /bɪ'haɪnd/
bit /bɪt/
bridge /brɪdʒ/
bus station /'bʌs ˌsteɪʃən/
bus stop /'bʌs ˌstɒp/
Can you tell me how to get to …? /ˌkən ju: tel mi: 'haʊ tə get tə/
canal /kə'næl/
castle /kɑ:sl/
cat /kæt/
centre /'sentə(r)/
cigarette /sɪgə'ret/
cinema /'sɪnəmə/
collect /kə'lekt/
cross the road /ˌkrɒs ðə 'rəʊd/
down /daʊn/
drop /drɒp/
entrance /'entrəns/
factory /'fæktrɪ/
field /fi:ld/
get to /'get tu:, tə/
gorgeous /'gɔ:dʒəs/
hairdresser /'heədresə(r)/
hobby /'hɒbɪ/
hurt /hɜ:t/
in a valley /ɪn ə 'vælɪ/
in front of /ɪn 'frʌnt əv/
in love /ɪn 'lʌv/
Is there much to do? /'ɪz ðeə ˌmʌtʃ tə 'du:/
knee /ni:/
ladder /'lædə(r)/
library /'laɪbrərɪ/
marsh /mɑ:ʃ/
mend /mend/
move in /ˌmu:v 'ɪn/
newsagent /'nju:zˌeɪdʒənt/
on one side of … /ɒn 'wʌn saɪd əv/
on the corner /ɒn ðə 'kɔ:nə(r)/
on the left /ɒn ðə 'left/
on the opposite side of … /ɒn ðɪ 'ɒpəzɪt saɪd əv/
over /'əʊvə(r)/
over here /ˌəʊvə 'hɪə(r)/
over there /ˌəʊvə 'ðeə(r)/
pack /pæk/
parade /pə'reɪd/
petrol station /'petrəl ˌsteɪʃən/
place /pleɪs/
pub /pʌb/
railway /'reɪlweɪ/
railway line /'reɪlweɪ ˌlaɪn/
river /'rɪvə/

round here /ˌraʊnd 'hɪə/
round the corner /ˌraʊnd
 ðə 'kɔːnə(r)/
secondary school /'sekəndrɪ
 ˌskuːl/
sheep /ʃiːp/
ship /ʃɪp/
shopping centre /'ʃɒpɪŋ
 ˌsentə(r)/
show somebody around
 /ˌʃəʊ ˌsʌmbɒdɪ ə'raʊnd/
spanner /'spænə(r)/
stamps /stæmps/
station /'steɪʃən/
tunnel /'tʌnəl/
turn /tɜːn/
turning /'tɜːnɪŋ/
valley /'vælɪ/

## UNIT 4 REVISION

autograph /'ɔːtəgraːf/
boxer /'bɒksə(r)/
charity /'tʃærətɪ/
contestant /kən'testənt/
cook (n.) /kʊk/
customer /'kʌstəmə(r)/
event /ɪ'vent/
hairdresser /'heədresə/
idea /aɪ'dɪə/
international /ɪntə'næʃnəl/
kiss /kɪs/
per cent /pə'sent/
personality /ˌpɜːsə'nælətɪ/
quiz /kwɪz/
round (n.) /raʊnd/
score /skɔː(r)/
sign /saɪn/
unusual /ʌn'juːʒʊəl/
writer /'raɪtə(r)/

## UNIT 5 TRAVEL

Africa /'æfrɪkə/
airport /'eəpɔːt/
Antarctica /æn'taːktɪkə/
Asia /'eɪʒə/
Australasia /ˌɒstrə'leɪʒə/
autumn /'ɔːtəm/
back /bæk/
boating lake /'bəʊtɪŋ ˌleɪk/
carry /'kærɪ/
clothes /kləʊðz/
continent /'kɒntɪnənt/
coast /kəʊst/
culture /'kʌltʃə/
destroy /dɪ'strɔɪ/
east /iːst/
educational /edʒə'keɪʃənəl/
environment /en'vaɪrəmənt/
Europe /'jʊərəp/
excited /ɪk'saɪtɪd/
expedition /ekspə'dɪʃən/
extra /'ekstrə/
fare /feə(r)/
famous /'feɪməs/
forever /fə'revə(r)/
fun fair /'fʌn feə(r)/

group /gruːp/
hire /'haɪə(r)/
holiday /'hɒlɪdeɪ/
homesick /'həʊmsɪk/
hot /hɒt/
How will I get to ...? /'haʊ
 wɪl aɪ ˌget tə/
include /ɪŋ'kluːd/
in the country /ɪn ðə 'kʌntrɪ/
Japan /dʒə'pæn/
journey /'dʒɜːnɪ/
learn /lɜːn/
luggage /'lʌgɪdʒ/
mechanic /mə'kænɪk/
meet /miːt/
member /'membə/
money /'mʌnɪ/
North America /ˌnɔːθ
 ə'merɪkə/
north /nɔːθ/
on my own /ˌɒn maɪ 'əʊn/
panic /'pænɪk/
passport /'paːspɔːt/
planet /'plænɪt/
provide /prə'vaɪd/
replace /rə'pleɪs/
return /rɪ'tɜːn/
save /seɪv/
scientist /'saɪəntɪst/
seaside /'siːsaɪd/
sightseeing /'saɪtsiːɪŋ/
single /'sɪŋgəl/
South America /ˌsaʊθ
 ə'merɪkə/
south /saʊθ/
Spain /speɪn/
Spanish /'spænɪʃ/
special /'speʃəl/
spring /sprɪŋ/
summer /'sʌmə(r)/
sunbathe /'sʌnbeɪð/
support /sə'pɔːt/
team /tiːm/
the Antarctic /ðɪ æn'taːktɪk/
the Arctic /ðɪ 'aːktɪk/
the Atlantic Ocean /ðɪ
 ət,læntɪk 'əʊʃən/
the Earth /ðɪ 'ɜːθ/
the Equator /ðɪ ɪ'kweɪtə(r)/
the Internet /ðiː 'ɪntənet/
the North Pole /ðə ,nɔːθ
 'pəʊl/
the Pacific Ocean /ðə
 pə,sɪfɪk 'əʊʃən/
the South Pole /ðə ,saʊθ
 'pəʊl/
ticket /'tɪkɪt/
train /treɪn/
travel /'trævəl/
trip /trɪp/
uncle /'ʌŋkəl/
vehicle /'viːɪkl/
visit /'vɪzɪt/
west /west/
What a pity! /ˌwɒt ə 'pɪtɪ/
winter /'wɪntə(r)/
wonderful /'wʌndəfʊl/

## UNIT 6 PROBLEMS

ambulance /'æmbjʊləns/
anywhere /'enɪweə(r)/
arm /aːm/
as ... /əz/
at the back of /ət ðə 'bæk əv/
aunt /aːnt/
bone /bəʊn/
chase /tʃeɪs/
chat (n.) /tʃæt/
climb down /ˌklaɪm 'daʊn/
climb up /ˌklaɪm 'ʌp/
crash /kræʃ/
cupboard /'kʌbəd/
cut (n) /kʌt/
everybody /'evrɪbɒdɪ/
everything /'evrɪθɪŋ/
everywhere /'evrɪweə(r)/
fall off /ˌfɔːl 'ɒf/
for a long time /fər ə ˌlɒŋ
 'taɪm/
forehead /'fɔːhed/
get dark /get 'daːk/
get off (a bus, train) /get
 'ɒf/
get on (a bus, train) /get
 'ɒn/
gran /græn/
head /hed/
idiot /'ɪdɪət/
insist /ɪn'sɪst/
in the opposite direction
 /ɪn ðɪ ,ɒpəzɪt daɪ'rekʃən/
It serves him right /ɪt ,sɜːvz
 hɪm 'raɪt/
just /dʒʌst/
just in time /ˌdʒʌst ɪn 'taɪm/
land (v.) /lænd/
magazine /mægə'ziːn/
memory /'memərɪ/
nobody /'nəʊbɒdɪ/
noise /nɔɪz/
nowhere /'nəʊweə(r)/
one-way street /ˌwʌn weɪ
 'striːt/
opposite direction /'ɒpəsɪt
 də'rekʃən/
packet /'pækɪt/
party /'paːtɪ/
pick up /'pɪk ʌp/
pocket /'pɒkɪt/
put /pʊt/
quarter of an hour
 /ˌkwɔːtər əv ən 'aʊə(r)/
realize /'rɪəlaɪz/
rescue /'reskjuː/
scar /skaː/
scratch /skrætʃ/
scream /skriːm/
settee /se'tiː/
shelf /ʃelf/
shoplift /'ʃɒplɪft/
smoke (v.) /sməʊk/
somebody /'sʌmbɒdɪ/
someone /'sʌmwʌn/
somewhere /'sʌmweə(r)/
souvenirs /suːvə'nɪəz/
speed up /ˌspiːd 'ʌp/

stand /stænd/
steal /stiːl/
stitch /stɪtʃ/
stool /stuːl/
stroke /strəʊk/
the other side of /ðə 'ʌðə
 saɪd əv/
under /'ʌndə(r)/
upset /ʌp'set/
village /'vɪlɪdʒ/
wave (v.) /weɪv/

## UNIT 7 COMPARISONS

a couple of /ə 'kʌpəl əv/
article /'aːtɪkəl/
as ... as ... /əz ... əz/
attractive /ə'træktɪv/
back to front /ˌbæk tə
 'frʌnt/
baggy /'bægɪ/
baseball cap /'beɪsbɔːl ˌkæp/
beard /bɪəd/
best /best/
better /'betə(r)/
blouse /blaʊz/
boot /buːt/
borrow /'bɒrəʊ/
bra /braː/
bust /bʌst/
casual /'kæʒʊəl/
century /'sentʃərɪ/
colourful /'kʌləfʊl/
comfortable /'kʌmftəbəl/
common /'kɒmən/
department store
 /dɪ'paːtmənt ˌstɔː(r)/
elephant /'elɪfənt/
fashion /'fæʃən/
fashionable /'fæʃnəbəl/
fault /fɒlt/
figure /'fɪgə(r)/
haircut /'heəkʌt/
hat /hæt/
heel /hiːl/
high /haɪ/
hippy /'hɪpɪ/
in fashion /ɪn 'fæʃən/
introduction /ˌɪntrə'dʌkʃən/
jumper /'dʒʌmpə(r)/
knee /niː/
knickers /'nɪkəz/
leg /leg/
lend /lend/
loose /luːs/
lovely /'lʌvlɪ/
make up /'meɪk ʌp/
maxi-dress /'mæksiːdres/
miniskirt /'mɪnɪskɜːt/
modern /'mɒdən/
moustache /mə'staːʃ/
much /mʌtʃ/
narrow /'nærəʊ/
pardon /'paːdən/
pink /pɪŋk/
pointed /'pɔɪntɪd/
popular /'pɒpjʊlə(r)/
punk /pʌŋk/

quid /kwɪd/
shopping /'ʃɒpɪŋ/
shorts /ʃɔ:ts/
sick /sɪk/
size /saɪz/
slim /slɪm/
smile /smaɪl/
sports clothes /'spɔ:ts
    kləʊðz/
stiff /stɪf/
stiletto /stɪ'letəʊ/
straight /streɪt/
suit /su:t/
tight /taɪt/
tights /taɪts/
to pay back /tə ,peɪ 'bæk/
toe /təʊ/
trainers /'treɪnəz/
true /tru:/
try on /traɪ 'ɒn/
underpants /'ʌndəpænts/
vest /vest/
vote (n. and v.) /'vəʊt/
waist /weɪst/
Who are you kidding?
    /'hu: ɑ: ju: ,kɪdɪŋ/
wide /waɪd/
winner /'wɪnə(r)/
worse /wɜ:s/
worst /wɜ:st/

## UNIT 8  VISITORS

all over /ɔ:l 'əʊvə(r)/
by your side /,baɪ jɔ: 'saɪd/
description /də'skrɪpʃən/
false /fɒls/
immediately /ɪ'mi:dɪətli:/
glad /glæd/
motorbike /'məʊtəbaɪk/
robbery /'rɒbərɪ/
sorrow /'sɒrəʊ/
take off /,teɪk 'ɒf/
taxi /'tæksɪ/
yours /jɔ:z/

## UNIT 9  VISITORS

astronomy /ə'strɒnəmɪ/
base /beɪs/
battle /'bætəl/
been /bi:n/
bell /bel/
British /'brɪtɪʃ/
brought /brɔ:t/
built /bɪlt/
butterfly /'bʌtəflaɪ/
cafeteria /kæfə'tɪərɪə/
calendar /'kæləndə(r)/
clock tower /'klɒk ,taʊə(r)/
close (adj.) /kləʊs/
collection /kə'lekʃən/
constable /'kʌnstəbəl/
contain /kən'teɪn/
county /'kaʊntɪ/
cousin /'kʌzən/
cowboy /'kaʊbɔɪ/
crown /kraʊn/
destroy /dɪ'strɔɪ/

dinosaur /'daɪnəsɔ:(r)/
display /dɪ'spleɪ/
done /dʌn/
bin /bɪn/
embarrassed /ɪm'bærəst/
execution /,eksɪ'kju:ʃən/
farm /fa:m/
get back /get 'bæk/
gift /gɪft/
go dead /gəʊ 'ded/
gone /gɒn/
Good Lord! /,gʊd 'lɔ:d/
got /gɒt/
had /hæd/
heard /hɜ:d/
hemisphere /'hemɪsfɪə/
Houses of Parliament
    /,haʊzɪz əv 'pɑ:ləmənt/
huge /hju:ʤ/

including /ɪŋ'klu:dɪŋ/
introduce /ɪntrə'dju:s/
jewel /ʤu:əl/
light /laɪt/
met /met/
mine (n.) /maɪn/
model /'mɒdəl/
most of /'məʊst əv/
mountain /'maʊntɪn/
observatory /əb'sɜ:vətrɪ/
official /ə'fɪʃəl/
on patrol /,ɒn pə'trəʊl/
only just /,əʊnlɪ 'ʤʌst/
palace /'pælɪs/
paper round /'peɪpə raʊnd/
patrol /pə'trəʊl/
plant (n.) /pla:nt/
police station /pə'li:s
    ,steɪʃən/
Prime Minister /,praɪm
    'mɪnɪstə(r)/
royal /'rɔɪəl/
search /sɜ:ʧ/
See you around /,si: ju:
    ə'raʊnd/
seen /si:n/
since /sɪns/
skeleton /'skelɪtən/
telescope /'telɪskəʊp/
the States /ðə 'steɪts/
thief /θi:f/
thrown /θrəʊn/
UFO /,ju: ef 'əʊ/
unpack /ʌn'pæk/
whale /weɪl/
zoo /zu:/

## UNIT 10  FOOD

alcoholic /,ælkə'hɒlɪk/
alternative /ɒl'tɜ:nətɪv/
anchovy /'ænʧəvɪ/
appetite /'æpɪtaɪt/
beans /bi:nz/
beef /bi:f/
beer /bɪə(r)/
bottle /'bɒtəl/
bowl /bəʊl/

bread /bred/
breadcrumbs /'bredkrʌmz/
broke /brəʊk/
bun /bʌn/
cake /keɪk/
carrot /'kærət/
carton /'ka:tən/
cheese /ʧi:z/
cheesecake /'ʧi:zkeɪk/
chicken /'ʧɪkɪn/
childish /'ʧaɪldɪʃ/
chillies /'ʧɪlɪz/
chips /ʧɪps/
chop /ʧɒp/
clove of garlic /,kləʊv əv
    'ga:lɪk/
coffee /'kɒfɪ/
Could we have ...? /'kʊd
    wɪ ,hæv/
cream /kri:m/
crisps /krɪsps/
cucumber /'kju:kʌmbə(r)/
customer /'kʌstəmə/
delicious /dɪ'lɪʃəs/
dessert /dɪ'zɜ:t/
diet /'daɪət/
drug store /'drʌg stɔ:(r)/
exotic /ɪg'zɒtɪk/
finally /'faɪnəlɪ/
fork /fɔ:k/
French fries /'frenʧ fraɪz/
fridge /frɪʤ/
fruit /fru:t/
fry /fraɪ/
garlic /'ga:lɪk/
gas /gæs/
glass /gla:s/
grill /grɪl/
ham /hæm/
Haven't you heard?
    /,hævənt ju: 'hɜ:d/
healthy /'helθɪ/
home-made /,həʊm 'meɪd/
information /,ɪnfə'meɪʃən/
ingredients /ɪn'gri:dɪənts/
instructions /ɪn'strʌkʃənz/
iron (n.) /'aɪən/
jacket potato /,ʤækɪt
    pə'teɪtəʊ/
leather /'leðə(r)/
lemon /'lemən/
lemonade /lemən'eɪd/
lettuce /'letɪs/
lift /lɪft/
loaf /ləʊf/
meat /mi:t/
milk /mɪlk/
minced /mɪnst/
mineral water /'mɪnrəl
    ,wɔ:tə(r)/
mix /mɪks/
mixture /'mɪksʧə/
motorway /'məʊtəweɪ/
mouth /maʊθ/
mushroom /'mʌʃru:m/
mussels /'mʌsəlz/
nuts /nʌts/
olives /'ɒlɪvz/
onion /'ʌnjən/

packet /'pækɪt/
pancake /'pæŋkeɪk/
pants /pænts/
paper /'peɪpə(r)/
peel /pi:l/
pepper /'pepə(r)/
peppers /'pepəz/
pie /paɪ/
pineapple /'paɪnæpəl/
pizza /'pi:tsə/
plastic /'plæstɪk/
potato /pə'teɪtəʊ/
pure /pjʊə(r)/
recipe /'resəpɪ/
refrigerator /rɪ'frɪʤəreɪtə(r)/
salad /'sæləd/
salad bar /'sæləd ba:(r)/
salami /sə'la:mɪ/
salt /sɒlt/
sardine /sa:'di:n/
sauce /sɔ:s/
sausage /'sɒsɪʤ/
see for yourself /,si: fə
    jɔ'self/
serve /sɜ:v/
shampoo /ʃæm'pu:/
slice /slaɪs/
soap powder /'səʊp
    ,paʊdə(r)/
soup /su:p/
starter /'sta:tə(r)/
starvation /sta:'veɪʃən/
steak /steɪk/
sweetcorn /'swi:tkɔ:n/
tin /tɪn/
toast /təʊst/
tomato /tə'ma:təʊ/
topping /'tɒpɪŋ/
traditional /trə'dɪʃnəl/
truck /trʌk/
tube /tju:b/
wholemeal /'həʊlmi:l/
tuna /'tju:nə/
waitress /'weɪtrəs/
wine /waɪn/
wish (v.) /wɪʃ/
wood /wʊd/
worm /wɜ:m/

## UNIT 11
## COMMUNICATION

acoustic guitar /ə'ku:stɪk
    ,gɪta:/
advantages /æd'va:ntɪʤɪz/
album /'ælbəm/
amplifier /'æmplɪfaɪə/
battery /'bætərɪ/
camera /'kæmrə/
catalogue /'kætəlɒg/
broadcast /'brɔ:dka:st/
central /'sentrəl/
chart /ʧa:t/
check (v.) /ʧek/
code number /'kəʊd
    ,nʌmbə(r)/
compact disc /,kɒmpækt
    'dɪsk/
compete /kəm'pi:t/

control /kən'trəʊl/
copy (n. and v.) /'kɒpɪ/
create /kri:'eɪt/
develop /dɪ'veləp/
development /dɪ'veləpmənt/
disadvantage
   /dɪsəd'va:ntɪdʒ/
discover /dɪ'skʌvə(r)/
done /dʌn/
electronics /ɪlek'trɒnɪks/
energy /'enədʒɪ/
envelope /'envələʊp/
exposure /ek'spəʊʒə/
heavy metal /hevɪ 'metəl/
I'm stuck! /ˌaɪm 'stʌk/
instrument /'ɪnstrəmənt/
invent /ɪn'vent/
invite /ɪn'vaɪt/
keyboard /'ki:bɔ:d/
laboratory /lə'bɒrətrɪ/
laziness /'leɪzɪnəs/
main /meɪn/
microphone /'maɪkrəfəʊn/
orchestra /'ɔ:kestrə/
order /'ɔ:də/
overtake /əʊvə'teɪk/
party /'pɑ:tɪ/
pocket money /'pɒkɪt
   ˌmʌnɪ/
print /prɪnt/
printer /'prɪntə(r)/
process (n.) /'prəʊses/
produce /prə'dju:s/
producer /prə'dju:sə(r)/
properly /'prɒpəlɪ/
record (v.) /rɪ'kɔ:d/
release /rɪ'li:s/
remove /rɪ'mu:v/
replace /rɪ'pleɪs/
revolutionize /revə'lu:ʃənaɪz/
rocket /'rɒkɪt/
sales /seɪlz/
sent /sent/
sort (out) /ˌsɔ:t ('aʊt)/
speaker /'spi:kə/
store /stɔ:/
stuck /stʌk/
That's that! /ˌðæts 'ðæt/
tone /təʊn/
trip /trɪp/
triple /'trɪpl/
videotape /'vɪdɪəʊteɪp/
warn /wɔ:n/
Would you like a hand?
   /ˌwʊd ju: ˌlaɪk ə 'hænd/

**UNIT 12 REVISION**

alone /ə'ləʊn/
charm /tʃɑ:m/
direction /də'rektʃən/
jazz /dʒæz/
leather /'leðə/
observant /ɒb'zɜ:vənt/
relax /rɪ'læks/
serious /'sɪərɪəs/

# USEFUL SETS

## Personal pronouns and adjectives

| subject pronoun | object pronoun | possessive adjective |
| --- | --- | --- |
| I /aɪ/ | me /mi:/ | my /maɪ/ |
| you /ju:/ | you /ju:/ | your /jɔ:(r)/ |
| he /hi:/ | him /hɪm/ | his /hɪz/ |
| she /ʃi:/ | her /hɜ:(r)/ | her /hɜ:(r)/ |
| it /ɪt/ | it /ɪt/ | its /ɪts/ |
| we /wi:/ | us /ʌs/ | our /aʊə(r)/ |
| they /ðeɪ/ | them /ðem/ | their /ðeə(r)/ |

## Irregular verbs

| infinitive | past tense | past participle |
| --- | --- | --- |
| be /bi:/ | was /wəz/, /wɒz/ were /wə(r)/, /wɜ:(r)/ | been /bi:n/ |
| become /bɪ'kʌm/ | became /bɪ'keɪm/ | become /bɪ'kʌm/ |
| bend /bend/ | bent /bent/ | bent /bent/ |
| break /breɪk/ | broke /brəʊk/ | broken /'brəʊkən/ |
| bring /brɪŋ/ | brought /brɔ:t/ | brought /brɔ:t/ |
| burn /bɜ:n/ | burnt /bɜ:nt/ | burnt /bɜ:nt/ |
| buy /baɪ/ | bought /bɔ:t/ | bought /bɔ:t/ |
| catch /kætʃ/ | caught /kɔ:t/ | caught /kɔ:t |
| come /kʌm/ | came /keɪm/ | come /kʌm/ |
| do /də/, /du:/ | did /dɪd/ | done /dʌn/ |
| drive /draɪv/ | drove /drəʊv/ | driven /'drɪvən/ |
| eat /i:t/ | ate /eɪt/ | eaten /'i:tən/ |
| fall /fɔ:l/ | fell /fel/ | fallen /'fɔ:lən/ |
| feel /fi:l/ | felt /felt/ | felt /felt/ |
| fight /faɪt/ | fought /fɔ:t/ | fought /fɔ:t/ |
| find /faɪnd/ | found /faʊnd/ | found /faʊnd/ |
| fly /flaɪ/ | flew /flu:/ | flown /fləʊn/ |
| forget /fə'get/ | forgot /fə'gɒt/ | forgotten /fə'gɒtən/ |
| get /get/ | got /gɒt/ | got /gɒt/ |
| give /gɪv/ | gave /geɪv/ | given /'gɪvən/ |
| go /gəʊ/ | went /went/ | gone /gɒn/ |
| have /hæv/ | had /hæd/ | had /hæd/ |
| hear /hɪə(r)/ | heard /hɜ:d/ | heard /hɜ:d/ |
| hit /hɪt/ | hit /hɪt/ | hit /hɪt/ |
| hold /həʊld/ | held /held/ | held /held/ |
| know /nəʊ/ | knew /nju:/ | known /nəʊn/ |
| leave /li:v/ | left /left/ | left /left/ |
| lend /lend/ | lent /lent/ | lent /lent/ |
| meet /met/ | met /met/ | met /met |
| pay /peɪ/ | paid /peɪd/ | paid /peɪd/ |
| put /pʊt/ | put /pʊt/ | put /pʊt/ |
| read /ri:d/ | read /red/ | read /red/ |
| ride /raɪd/ | rode /rəʊd/ | ridden /'rɪdən/ |
| ring /rɪŋ/ | rang /ræŋ/ | rung /rʌŋ/ |
| run /rʌn/ | ran /ræn/ | run /rʌn/ |
| say /seɪ/ | said /sed/ | said /sed/ |
| see /si:/ | saw /sɔ:/ | seen /si:n/ |
| sell /sel/ | sold /səʊld/ | sold /səʊld/ |
| send /send/ | sent /sent/ | sent /sent/ |
| sink /sɪŋk/ | sank /sæŋk/ | sunk /sʌŋk/ |
| sit /sɪt/ | sat /sæt/ | sat /sæt/ |
| steal /sti:l/ | stole /stəʊl/ | stolen /'stəʊlən/ |
| take /teɪk/ | took /tʊk/ | taken /'teɪkən/ |
| think /θɪŋk/ | thought /θɔ:t/ | thought /θɔ:t/ |
| throw /θrəʊ/ | threw /θru:/ | thrown /θrəʊn/ |
| wake up /weɪk 'ʌp/ | woke up /wəʊk 'ʌp/ | woken up /wəʊkən 'ʌp/ |

# OXFORD
## UNIVERSITY PRESS

Great Clarendon Street, Oxford OX2 6DP

Oxford University Press is a department of the University of Oxford.
It furthers the University's objective of excellence in research, scholarship,
and education by publishing worldwide in

Oxford  New York

Auckland  Cape Town  Dar es Salaam  Hong Kong  Karachi
Kuala Lumpur  Madrid  Melbourne  Mexico City  Nairobi
New Delhi  Shanghai  Taipei  Toronto

With offices in

Argentina  Austria  Brazil  Chile  Czech Republic  France  Greece
Guatemala  Hungary  Italy  Japan  Poland  Portugal  Singapore
South Korea  Switzerland  Thailand  Turkey  Ukraine  Vietnam

OXFORD and OXFORD ENGLISH are registered trade marks of
Oxford University Press in the UK and in certain other countries

© Oxford University Press

The moral rights of the author have been asserted

Database right Oxford University Press (maker)

International edition
ISBN : 978 0 19 435759 3
First published 1998
2016  2015  2014  2013  2012
30  29  28  27  26  25

Turkish edition
ISBN : 978 0 19 435877 4
First published 1998
2004  2003  2002  2001  2000
10  9  8  7  6

### No unauthorized photocopying

Printed in China

ACKNOWLEDGEMENTS

The author would like to thank his wife, Eunice, and
his children without whose support and patience
*New Hotline* would not have been possible.

The author and publishers would also like to thank the
ELT teachers and advisers who have given generously
of their time to talk about their needs and *New Hotline*.

Special thanks are due to a panel of British teenagers,
Juliet Kinsman, Zuleika Melluish, Pema Radha, Alex
Huskinson and Mark Killingley, for their advice on the
Victoria Road storyline, and on the Reading and
Listening topics.

'Blue Suede Shoes', words and music by Carl Lee
Perkins, used by kind permission of Carlin Music
Corporation, Iron Bridge House, 3 Bridge Approach,
Chalk Farm, London NW1 8BD.

'Glad All Over' by Dave Clark and Mike Smith,
Copyright © 1963 Ivy Music Ltd., 8/9 Frith St, London
W1V 5TZ, England.
Reproduced by permission. All rights reserved.

*The publishers would like to thank the following for their permission
to reproduce photographs:*
Andes Press, Aquarius Picture Library, Catherine Blackie,
Bubbles, Collections, Chris Fairclough, Ford, S & R
Greenhill, Tom Hutchinson, Robert Harding Picture
Library, Image Bank, Rickenbaker, Retna Pictures, Rex
Features, Tony Stone, Telegraph Colour Library, Madame
Tussauds, John Walmsley, Zefa and the Stockmarket.

*Illustrations by*:
Phil Bannister, Brett Breckon, Stephan Chabluk, Chris
Chaisty, Paul Dickinson, Nicki Elson, Roger Fereday, Phil
Gascoine, James Griffiths, Michael Kumon, Claire
Littlejohn, Penny Sobr, Phil Smith, Tech Graphics, George
Turner, Harry Venning, Katharine Walker, Lis Watkins.

*Victoria Road photo story*: photography by John Walmsley

*Location photography by*: Rob Judges and Maggie Milner

*Studio photography by*: Pat Downing and Mark Mason

*The characters in Victoria Road were played by*:
Sarah Buckley, Matthew Christmas, Joseph Derrett,
Natalie Kowlessur, Tito Menezes, Robert Page, Graham
and Sue Page, Simon Richards, Paul and Pat Rose, Sarah
Rose, Patrick Short, Matthew Starling.

*The publishers would like to thank the following for their help
with the Victoria Road photo story*:
Ardmore Adventure Holidays; Banstead Sports Centre;
Cannon cinema, Ewell; Epsom and Ewell High School;
London and Country Buses; McDonalds; Met Police Public
Relations; Mrs Moretta; Frances Myers; NESCOT drama
department; One Stop Shop, Burgh Heath; Pickfords; St
Andrews School, Leatherhead; St David's School, Ashford;
Therfield School, Leatherhead; Thorndike Youth Theatre;
Rose and Brian Walsh; Whitgift Centre Croydon;
Worcester Park Football Club.